YOUR DAUGHTER'S NOT IN HEAVEN

Dorothy Houghton

Right Angle Publications

First published in 1996 by

Right Angle Publications

an Imprint of Right Angle Associates
18 Rainham Gardens
Ruddington
Nottingham
NG11 6HX

Cover illustration by Karen Stephens

ISBN 1-900570-00-9

I dedicate this book to my Godchildren.

ACKNOWLEDGEMENTS

I am most grateful for the support and encouragement I have had throughout the writing of this book.

My personal thanks go to Cathy Clark, who originally typed out the manuscript from longhand and greatly encouraged me when I was ready to throw the unfinished work in the bin, and to Reg Wyatt who edited the book for me.

I'm so grateful to my wonderful husband, Mike, for his tremendous help throughout its writing and for being responsible for getting the book into print. My thanks go to my super children, Sam and Emma, who have coped so well with me spending hours on the computer when they wanted to use it.

I am indebted to the people in the book who have given me permission to include them. For professional or personal reasons some have chosen to be referred to by a different name.

I'd also like to thank all the people who have read this book throughout its production and have been very kind and helpful in their comments. It has been a great help.

I thank God for it was He who told me to write the book in the first place.
I thank the Lord Jesus for enabling me to hear the voice of God.
I thank the Holy Spirit for helping me to remember the events as they happened.

4

CONTENTS

CHAPTER ONE

Sam

It was June 13th 1983, I was 32 weeks pregnant. We'd had a lovely weekend. We'd been to a friend's barbecue on the Saturday. On the Sunday we'd been to my brother John's for tea. And now it was Monday morning. I woke with a start. I'd wet myself, I couldn't understand it. I looked at the clock, 3.00 a.m. And then it dawned on me. I was horrified. I woke Mike. "My waters have gone. Something's gone wrong. Quick, Mike, 'phone for an ambulance." He fell out of bed, trying to wake up, and rushed downstairs. I just lay there not daring to move. Surely I can't be having the baby yet. Not yet. It's too soon. My poor baby. I was frightened." Please, God, don't let anything happen to my baby. Oh, Mum, I wish you were here. I want my Mum." Mike reappeared, "It's on its way. What's happened?" I explained how my waters had gone and that I dare not move. He fetched me a towel and helped me sit up. I stuffed the towel between my legs. What was I trying to do? Stop the baby from falling out? Mike sort of put my dressing gown on me and then proceeded to pack some things in a carrier bag. He dug out a booklet I'd been given from antenatal classes in which there was a list of things "for your suitcase". I was supposed to have got it ready. Blow all that - an ASDA bag was the nearest thing to hand. The ambulance arrived. They bundled me into it, with my carrier bag in one hand and my towel still held firmly by my other hand between my legs - and I wasn't going to let go of it. Mike followed us in the car.

The nearest hospital was the Queen's Medical Centre, Q.M.C. for short. It's a big teaching hospital in Nottingham. It's about three miles away from my home in the village of Ruddington. Once in the maternity suite, the powers that be decided to put me on a drip to try to stop the birth. They put a belt across my stomach with wires which connected me

7

up to a television screen. This monitored the baby's health. I lay there in shock with all these machines around me and a needle in me, just trying to come to terms with what was happening. The midwife tried to assure me that everything would be all right and I think that I believed her. But I wasn't really psyched up into being in hospital at that particular moment. I should have been at home, having a nice lie in. The only thing I'd been expecting to do was go to my third relaxation class that afternoon. Not much chance of that now! Mike sat there in shock too. We held hands, but didn't say much. What is there to say at a time like that? Everything seemed to be going fairly smoothly. At about 8.00 a.m. Mike decided to go home, have some breakfast and make a few 'phone calls. Then he came back to be with me. We said a fairly positive "Cheerio", but I think we both knew that we wanted to be with each other, to support each other.

I felt very alone once he'd gone. I suddenly felt vulnerable. I tried to get a bit of sleep. I may even have dozed off, I don't know. He was soon back, armed with some toiletries, clothes, magazines and food. He'd 'phoned work and told them he wouldn't be in that day. He'd 'phoned the health visitor to say that I wouldn't be in to relaxation. He'd bumped into my friend Liz in the village and she had asked him how I was. He'd felt sort of amused telling her that I was in hospital with my waters broken. The whole thing was strangely exciting, we didn't feel frightened. The midwife had done a good job of reassuring us. We were feeling fairly relaxed when the doctor arrived. He examined me and said that my cervix was opening. The baby wanted to be born and didn't want to stay inside me. It wasn't responding as it should have done to the drip. He changed tactics and selected a different drip. This one would actually help to induce the birth. That way, hopefully, the baby would come out easily, with no undue alarm. I was asked what form of pain relief I'd like to use. I opted for an epidural, because I'd heard that Pethidine could have some after-effects on the child. As for gas and air and breathing techniques, we were supposed to have been discussing them that afternoon at the ante - natal clinic....

So there we were, waiting. I'd been given my epidural and my drip had been changed. The midwife had said that it would all probably start happening at about three o'clock. She wasn't far wrong. They kept measuring my cervix. Everything was quite satisfactory. The Special Care Baby Unit, S.C.B.U. for short (pronounced sku-boo), had been informed that they would be receiving a new baby that afternoon. A paediatrician would be there at the birth. There was nothing to worry about. And then, at about two o'clock, things started to happen. The midwife decided to top up my epidural. It was starting to wear off and I was starting to feel contraction pains. I was a bit shocked and frightened at this, almost cross, in fact. I'd been told that having a child with an epidural was painless. I was told to start pushing. I tried to. Really hard. But it's difficult trying to push when what you are pushing with has been half numbed by an epidural. Plus the fact that when I pushed it hurt and I'd not been expecting any pain. Then there's the midwife telling me how to breathe, because I hadn't practised it. I felt completely at a loss. And there's Mike there, telling me to push, and I'm telling him that I *am* and that I'm in pain when I'm not supposed to be.

Suddenly the scanner started to show signs that the baby's heart was not as it should be. A doctor was summoned, a different one. "Right, we need to deliver this baby very soon. If you can't manage to get it out by yourself very soon, Dorothy, then we'll have to do it for you."

"Cold-hearted swine," I thought, "who are you anyway?" I pushed, or tried to push, again....nothing.

"Foetal distress," was called out by a nurse who was looking at the monitor. "Right, O.K. I'll take over," said the doctor. He started shouting orders and it looked like organised chaos was going on. Mike was told to stand to one side.

The doctor acted swiftly. He cut me and then with forceps, pulled my baby out. He dumped my baby on my tummy. "There you are," he said, "you've got a boy." I stared at the tiny form lying there. I didn't dare touch him. I looked at Mike, then back to my child. "It's...it's a baby!" I whispered. I couldn't believe it. I was in shock. I still didn't dare touch him.

The paediatrician was hovering impatiently. She waited a while and then picked him up and wrapped him in a blanket. Then she took him over to some apparatus at the far side of the room and did various "things" to him, I couldn't see what. Then she told me that she was going to take him to S.C.B.U. and that I could come and see him shortly. She disappeared whilst holding on to my baby. And that was it. He'd gone. I looked at Mike. We had a hug and a cry, of relief perhaps. We both felt weird. We'd had a baby when we hadn't been ready for it. We hadn't bought many

9

things. We hadn't got his bedroom ready. I hadn't read any books about being a Mum. Oh, yes... one. A friend had given me, "Breast is Best". That book was to make me very upset later on.

The doctor then began to sew me up. He sat there with his needle and thread, whistling away whilst he was sewing. "Do you always whistle whilst you're sewing people?", I had to ask him. He just seemed so oblivious to any decorum that I thought I deserved. Not that I felt anything special at that moment. In fact, I felt rather like a turkey being dressed. He made some sort of flippant comment that I probably deserved.

I was taken up on to the main maternity ward where I was put into a side ward. I thought that very kind of them. You see, on the main ward all the Mums had their babies in cots at the bottom of their beds. It was nice that I wasn't with them. It wasn't long before I was taken down to the Special Care Baby Unit. When we arrived there and went through the big swing doors it was like entering another world. There was machinery everywhere - monitors, screens, incubators. It all seemed so high-tech. And it was so very hot, like being in a greenhouse. Mike had taken me (escorted by a porter) in a wheelchair.

I was wheeled into the "hot" room. We were to discover later that there were two main rooms, a hot room and a cool room. Initially babies were taken to the hot room and then, eventually weaned into the cool room, before going home. We were shown to an incubator. There in it lay our son. Our Sam. Samuel James. We'd never had any doubts that our first son would be called Samuel James. Samuel after my Dad and James because Mike was christened Michael James, and his Dad had been christened Hedley James.

And there he was, in front of us. A tiny mite weighing in at 4lb 3oz, (1.900kg). He looked so frail, so defenceless. He had a bonnet and bootees on. Wires connected him to a machine. His face looked as if it had been hurt by the forceps. His right eye was virtually closed and heavily bruised. "Can I touch him?" I asked the doctor. "Yes, of course you can."

I opened a glass porthole and reached in. I touched his little hand. It was so tiny. I stroked it. I picked it up and balanced it on one of my fingers. I left it there, stroking it. It was then that I felt a tingly, goose-pimply feeling inside me. The little vulnerable life-form in front of me was my son. I'd just given birth to him. It was then that the full realisation of what had happened dawned on me. I was a Mum, Mike was a Dad. Sam was ours. It was here that Sam and I bonded. I wanted to pick him up and cuddle him... but I couldn't.

The paediatrician told us that things looked very good. We shouldn't really have to worry about him. He was in the best place, with excellent doctors and nurses to look after him. I was shown into the "milking room". Here I was shown the various contraptions that were to help me express my milk. It was explained to me that Sam would have to be given special milk for his first few days, after which he would be able to have my milk, once it had come. Sam would not have the strength to suck the milk from me. So he would be fed through a tube inserted up his nose. This tube went down into his stomach and the milk would be dripped into him. It all sounded very complicated, but I listened and tried to remember it all.

I was sent back onto the ward with a contraption called a breast pump. It resembled one of those measuring cylinders which I used to use during my chemistry lessons years ago. The principle was that I gently pulled at an outer cylinder, whilst holding on to an inner cylinder which was firmly pressed around my breast. The suction would cause the milk to express itself and collect in the outer cylinder. Mike thought it was really funny when I used this contraption and an automatic breast pump which was available in the "milking room". I felt as if I was a human cow with it clamped to my boobs. The things we women have to go through! It was rather a performance using it and there were many times when I felt like giving up and giving Sam a bottle of powdered milk instead. But, you see, I'd read this book called "Breast is Best", so I felt that I really should give my son the best milk he could possibly have, i.e. mine. It was a bit demoralising that my son was starting his life with bottled milk. I knew that it was special milk for premature babies, but I felt a bit of a failure.

I had quite a good night's sleep that first night I woke up eager to go and see how Sam was. I had to wait for what seemed ages before a porter finally took me down to S.C.B.U. I wasn't allowed to go down by myself. I had to go in a wheelchair. I was feeling rather sore around my bottom. It was hardly surprising! Again I was wheeled into this world of high technology. It must have cost tens of thousands of pounds. I went to say good morning to my baby. " 'Morning, Sam. It's your Mummy here. Are you all right?" As if he could understand!

The nurse told me that Sam had had a peaceful night and was doing well. They were hoping to get him out of the incubator later that day and into a cot. I stayed there as long as I could. I felt a bit in the way, but I wanted to be there to look at his beautiful little face, even though it was battered and bruised. His eye was still closed and bruised. He looked as if he'd been in a fight. We later nicknamed him Henry, after Henry Cooper, the boxer.

My poor Sam. Occasionally I'd put my hand in and hold his hand. It would instinctively curl round my finger. It had such long fingers and perfect nails. The finger nail on his little finger was absolutely minute, and yet perfect in every detail. Incredible. I could have sat there all day, just looking.

I had to go back onto the main ward for my meals and for the doctor's rounds. He seemed quite happy with me. They couldn't really give me a definite reason as to why Sam had been born prematurely. They had noted that my placenta had not been a very healthy colour, and it was quite possible that it had stopped functioning properly, which would have accounted for Sam wanting to be born early. He just wasn't getting any food. This failing of the placenta is not an uncommon cause of premature babies, I was told. The phrase "not uncommon" appeared in my life at this point. It became a regular feature during my times in hospital.

They took Sam out of the incubator, only to put him back in later. He wasn't ready yet to come out, they told me. Perhaps tomorrow. I felt quite good that day. I suppose that I was happy because now I was a Mum. A proud Mum.

Wednesday came and I didn't have such a good day. I was wheeled into S.C.B.U. to see Sam lying in the heat of a bright fluorescent light. He had a protective eye shield on. It frightened me. What was wrong with him? It was nothing serious, I was told. He'd got jaundice. Jaundice? What was that? It was quite common in premature babies, I was told. I panicked. I didn't know anything about jaundice. Back on the ward, I got out my big baby book and read all about it. I'd only finished work two weeks ago. Ask me a question about French, and I'd be O.K.. That, after all was my job - a French teacher. But now I was a Mum, with a new job. I needed to read up on it.

On Thursday they switched off the heat lamp. On Friday it was back on again.

Saturday was Mike's big day. He fed Sam. He sat there with Sam in his arms and held the syringe with the milk in it, and let it drip slowly into his son's stomach. It was lovely to sit and watch them. I'm sure it helped Mike to bond so well with Sam. The idea of breast feeding is good, but I think that hubby can feel left out of it. Sam couldn't yet cope with my breast, which was still a bit of a blow for me. However, it did mean that the two men could have an intimate relationship. It all seemed very healthy.

Sunday was Fathers' Day. By now I was allowed to walk around the hospital quite freely during the day-time, so I'd no problems getting Mike a card from the hospital shop. It had something on it like, "Life has lots of little surprises", which we both felt was most apt. On that day the light was switched off for the last time. Sam's jaundice had cleared up. He also came out of the incubator. He was six days old.

Things were looking good. By now my milk had well and truly come and I was filling bottles for Sam with no problem at all. I was actually producing too much milk for him and so was able to give some to a new Mum on my ward who'd given birth to a huge baby boy. Her milk hadn't come yet. She was feeling a bit of a failure too. Life's like that sometimes, isn't it?

My bottom was still giving me problems. I was very bruised and had to have a ring cushion to sit on. It was like a round cushion with the middle missing, rather like a Polo mint. I went everywhere with it. When the nurse had taken my stitches out she was rather surprised at the number there were. The whistling doctor had a lot to answer for. I had salt baths and ice packs to try and ease the pain. It was so painful! I'm sure that this wasn't described in any of my books. I was quite well physically, compared to some other mothers who'd had babies the same day that I had Sam. That was because I was forever going down to S.C.B.U. I was known as the lady in the conspicuous bright yellow dressing gown, clinging to her "whoopee cushion". I certainly wasn't going to leave that around. I was also wearing a white elastic bandage on my right leg because a tremendous varicose vein had appeared. I must have walked along those corridors at least a dozen times a day, to-ing and fro-ing.

It was Monday, Sam was one week old. He was moved into the cool room. Marvellous. First he was put into a cot with no lid on. Then it was decided that he needed the lid on. Then it was decided that he should have an extra blanket. Finally that day they decided that it would be all right to have the lid off. The "lid" was a plastic canopy which just rested on top of the plastic cot. It was there for extra warmth.

By now all of our immediate family had been to see Sam except my sister Margaret who lived at that time in Manchester. I'd kept in touch with her via the telephone. It had been great fun 'phoning people up and telling them the news. It's nice giving people happy news when they're not expecting it.

Sam was doing well. His bruising had gone quite a lot and his eye didn't look so awful. It took almost two weeks for the bruise to go completely. Some nurses had commented that the Neville Barnes forceps used can be a bit brutal. He was still being fed through the tube up his nose. What we eventually did was put my milk in a bottle and feed him that way. An extra long teat was used to make it easier for him. By the age of two weeks Sam was being bottle fed, and the tube was abandoned.

On day ten, I came home. It was with mixed feelings. I'd had enough of being on the main ward, where the routine was beginning to get to me. I'd have liked to stay with Sam, but they couldn't accommodate me down on S.C.B.U. They did have a parenting room next to S.C.B.U. but that was reserved for mums who were going to take their baby home the next day. They could experience in hospital an entire night with their baby. I could look forward to my turn, probably within the next two weeks. It was nice to go home, to be alone with Mike again. But it seemed strange without a baby. It all seemed like a dream. Mike had been working wonders with Sam's bedroom. He'd painted it and it looked great. True, the carpet had yet to come, but it was delivered in time for Sam's homecoming.

I went into hospital every day to do Sam's "cares", as they were called, i.e., to wash and bathe him. I timed my arrival so that I could give him a feed or two. The nurses were super with me. I did feel so inadequate at times. I felt so silly that here I was - 31 years of age and I was all fingers and thumbs trying to bath my baby. But perhaps lots of new mothers are like that. I don't know. I remember the first time that I bathed Sam I ended up in tears because I couldn't seem to hold him as firmly as the nurses, and I could sense that Sam wasn't feeling so confident with me.

It was good fun shopping. I'd bought nothing so far. Only what friends had sold us second-hand. I now knew what I needed to get. Lots of premature baby clothes. And I had the time to do it, because I didn't have my baby with me.

14

I was still quite merrily pumping away on the old breast pump. Mike still found it fascinating. I suppose it was really. I'd get up in the night to get rid of some more milk. I was given loads of tiny bottles by S.C.B.U. on which I labelled the time the milk was expressed. That way they knew which to use first.

When Sam was three weeks old, he came home. He was taking my milk from a bottle, no problem, and was putting on weight at a very healthy rate. When we brought him home, we felt quite awestruck that there were only the two of us to look after him. No nurses and doctors hovering, just us. We'd become so used to having lots of people around Sam. Now there weren't any.

We were concerned that we had brought him from a virtually sterile environment to our home. We thought that we ought perhaps to continue washing our hands before we touched him, just for a few days, and asked visitors to do so as well. We'd had to "scrub-up" before we'd been able to touch Sam whilst he was in S.C.B.U. It seemed only right to continue with this habit.

Life was super. July was glorious. Sam was fine. The pump was still doing it's job, though I did get a bit fed up with it at times. It seemed a long performance - me expressing the milk then putting it into a bottle and giving it to Sam. But it continued only for three weeks or so. I eventually weaned him onto a nipple shield - yet another marvellous invention. It was like a big teat which was fitted over my nipple and then placed into Sam's mouth. Great.

We were having to set the alarm at night to wake me up every four hours to feed Sam. He could not give an audible cry and needed to be fed regularly. I'm sure that this contributed to Sam being such a contented baby. He didn't have to cry for his food at all. And he *was* a contented baby. Why shouldn't he be? He had two parents who really idolised him. We thought he was great. We thought it was funny how we stopped calling each other Mike and Dot and started using Mummy and Daddy instead.

He was duly christened at three months in the Houghton heirloom christening gown, on Sunday 8th September - I had to look that up in my diary. It's not a date that I remember. I wonder if other people do? I'm a godmother to some of my nieces and nephews, but I can't remember which ones, nor the dates of their christening.

15

We'd had a long chat about Sam's christening with the vicar. You see, Mike and I weren't exactly in agreement about it. I definitely wanted Sam to be christened, because all my family had been "done". We always had a family get-together and a big "do". I couldn't have imagined *not* getting Sam christened. In my opinion, it was the right thing to do. You have a child and you get him or her christened. Now Mike was of a different opinion. He didn't know whether he wanted Sam to be christened. He wondered if we should wait until Sam was old enough to choose for himself. Mike had been christened when he was eleven years old, because his parents were moving around so much that they just hadn't had a chance to make arrangements. So we thought we'd seek the vicar's advice on it. So, on Wednesday 17th August 1983, we sat in his lounge and asked him what his opinion was. He told us that, in his opinion, a child couldn't have a better start in life than by being christened. He felt it the right thing to do.

We then talked about godparents. Mike and I here were of the same opinion, but it was different to the vicar's. We both felt that if anybody was going to take charge of Sam's Christian upbringing, then it would be us, the parents, not some aunt or uncle who only saw Sam twice a year. We wanted ourselves to be his godparents. The vicar explained that it was customary to have three godparents, two male and one female or one male and two female depending on the sex of the godchild, those godparents not being the actual parents. We didn't want to partake of this custom. It didn't seem right for us. All my family lived quite a way from me and I didn't see them very often at all. It really did make more sense to us that *we* should be Sam's godparents.

The vicar left it with us to decide. He did hope that we might consider at least one other person to be a godparent, to make the numbers up to three. We thanked him, went home, mulled it over and decided that we'd stick at two. Here I have to confess that I am a godparent to two of my nieces, but I have *never* done anything at all about their Christian upbringing. I've never really felt that it was required of me by their parents or by myself. I'd assumed, perhaps wrongly, that they would not have wanted me poking my nose into whether their child was going to church or Sunday school or Junior church, or whatever else it might be called. I suppose that I could have bought them a Bible or some Christian books. But I haven't. To me, sadly now in hindsight, it was just a tradition. It was something that happened automatically once a child was born and I never really thought about it very deeply. It was purely a naming ceremony and an excuse for a get-together and a booze-up. It had no deep spiritual meaning to me, like it does nowadays. But then again, at that time, I was spiritually dead.

CHAPTER TWO

Lydia

It was Saturday, 7th December, 1985. I was 16 weeks pregnant and I was in hospital. But this wasn't a rush job and I wasn't in any danger. Or at least, I didn't think I was. We'd been "trying" (Mike hates that word) for another baby for quite some time. It actually took 14 months for me to conceive and, although that may not seem a long time to you, believe me, when you really want a child, 14 months is a very long time. I had, in fact, been going to the fertility clinic to see if there was anything wrong. Sam's prematurity had made me wonder if something was, perhaps, not quite right with my body. However, I was 16 weeks pregnant. Hurray! Sam was two and a half and full of energy and a real bundle of fun. I was very happy.

The gynaecologist had decided that the neck of my womb was weaker than it should be, and so intended to, as it were, sew it up, in an attempt to stop another premature birth. The technical phraseology was a Shirodkar Suture. And that's why I was in hospital, to be sewn up. The plan was that I go in on Saturday, be "done" on the Sunday and go home on the Monday. When I arrived I was told I'd been misinformed. It was to be the operation on Monday and home, perhaps, on Wednesday, but most probably, Thursday. Mike and I looked at each other in horror. He'd booked to have only the Monday off work. But there was nothing we could do. Mike went home to try and get things sorted out.

I was duly "sewn up", the operation being a fairly uncomplicated one. When I came to, the nurse told me to tell her if I felt any uncomfortable pains in my stomach. She went away. I started to get some awful tightening pains. They really hurt. The baby was quite active. My stomach felt as if was contracting badly. I called for the nurse, not realising what was happening.

"My stomach's hurting. It keeps...well, like tightening up, and my back's hurting." I still hadn't grasped what was going on. The nurse dashed off. She came back with someone else. I was instructed to take some tablets, which would stop it all. And I lay there, with this tightening in my stomach, thinking "What's going on? I've never felt pains like this before." And then I thought, "Yes I have. It was when the epidural was wearing off when I gave birth to Sam." They were like labour pains. Then the full horror of what was happening dawned on me. I was having contractions. My baby was trying to be born, at *16 weeks*. My body was trying to miscarry. Goodness! I couldn't believe it. I hadn't expected this. I hadn't been told that this could happen. I wasn't going to lose my baby now, was I? Not after all this waiting and wanting, surely not. I lay there frightened. Very frightened. I hardly dare move. I wanted Mike. Where was he? At home with Sam. I needed help. Help me, please someone. Don't let me lose my baby. My daughter.

I had the same gut feeling that the baby inside me was a girl that I'd had when I felt that Sam would be a boy. As someone had pointed out to me, I had a 50:50 chance of being right. But I knew, don't ask me how, but I did. And I did so want this little girl. I couldn't wait to have her. We were going to have such a wonderful time together. I was going to do all the things that mothers do with daughters. I wanted to so much. Especially because I felt I'd missed out on it all through my Mum's early death. She'd died of cancer when I was five. My daughter and I were going to have such a wonderful time. And I was contracting. Life wasn't fair. Please, God, don't let me lose this baby. Please.

Things started to settle down. The tablets were working, thank God. I had to continue to take them for quite a while. I can't remember how long, exactly. It was something like two weeks. They stopped the miscarriage. They had one very big side effect. Within half an hour of taking the tablet - Ritodrine - I felt as if I was having a heart attack. My heart would beat much faster than usual, making me incapable of doing anything. I just had to sit or lie down. I did eventually come to terms with it, but sometimes it was difficult with a two and a half year old to care for. I remember when I had to drive the car after taking a tablet. I'd had no choice but to do so. And it was an absolute nightmare, driving from the hospital to Radcliffe on Trent, about six miles, with my heart feeling that it was going to explode. But I managed it.

19

So ended my short stay in hospital. I had thought that my next stay there would be in May, because the expected date of the birth was May 25th. But it was not to be. Life always seems to have its unexpected surprises, waiting, hiding, ready to spring out on you when you're not ready.

It was Monday 17th March 1986, 5.15 a.m.. I woke up with a start. My waters had broken, there seemed to be gallons of it. "Oh no," I groaned, "not again. Quick, Mike, a towel, my waters have gone." He leapt out of bed and grabbed a towel from the bathroom. I pushed it between my legs. We sat there, or rather I lay there and he sat there, both with looks of despair and confusion written all over our faces. We weren't ready for this - not *ten* weeks early. We thought we'd be all right this time. So much for the Shirodkar Suture! No good at all, was it? Now what do we do? Mike was trying to collect his thoughts. "I'll ring for an ambulance then get your things ready." He went downstairs while I lay there thinking crazy thoughts, silly unimportant things like "I didn't get round to putting a waterproof sheet on the bed to protect the mattress, I hope I haven't ruined it. What was I going to do about Sam? I'm supposed to be going to relaxation today." I don't think I really thought about the baby inside me. I didn't even consider that anything could be wrong with her. Talk about being naive.

Mike came back upstairs, "The ambulance is on its way." He dug out a carrier bag and quickly threw in a few things - nightie, toothbrush, comb, talc, towel, soap, just the basics. The ambulance arrived. Mike said he'd wait until a reasonable time and then 'phone his Mum and Dad and ask them to come through and look after Sam, so he'd be able to come and join me. So off I toddled into the ambulance, clutching my towel in between my legs and clinging on to my carrier bag. Mike saw me disappearing into the morning mist yet again in an ambulance with its blue flashing lights. Poor old Mike.

When I got to the hospital it was decided to try and leave the baby inside me for as long as possible - the theory being that the longer she was inside me, the more she'd grow. However, there was the possibility that the baby might get an infection, since she was no longer protected by the amniotic fluid in the sac.

Mike arrived at about 8.00 a.m. His parents, Mercia and Lofty, were looking after Sam. Nature, however decided to have its way and I started to have contractions. They measured me and decided that the best thing to do was to let the baby be born. At about twelve, the nurse told Mike that he could go home, have some lunch and come back at about three o'clock. He'd be O.K., he wouldn't miss anything. I didn't want him to leave me. I felt that the nurse was wrong in her judgement, but here were the experts saying everything was fine, and who was I to question their knowledge about the time my baby would be born? So I didn't say anything and off Mike went. My contractions grew worse. They hurt, but in some strange, masochistic way they're a sheer delight because you know they're part and parcel of getting near to having that much wanted baby in your arms.

The baby was feet down and had been ever since I had first been examined. The doctor tried to turn her round several times but couldn't. And then things suddenly started happening. A leg had appeared and they were trying to push it back up. I was contracting badly. The nurse was saying to me "Don't push, don't push," and I didn't want to push or harm my baby, but something inside me definitely *did* want me to push, it was really hard for me not to. "Foetal distress" was suddenly announced, "It'll have to be a section. Quick, get her to surgery." It was organised chaos around me - one nurse had suddenly grabbed a razor and was shaving me, apologising because she was having to be so rough. Another was asking me if I had any crowns or dentures. Another was taping my rings to me. All this happened in a minute or two. I could feel things happening inside me. I could feel my baby trying to get out. I could feel a foot poking out. It was weird, but beautiful. After all, it was my baby's foot. Where's Mike, I want Mike here. They started wheeling me quickly down a corridor. I saw a figure at the other end. It was Mike. I felt a great sense of relief. Something was tickling me in between my legs - our baby's foot. Oh it won't be long now,

Mike was asking a nurse, "What's going on? What's happening?"

"The baby's got foetal distress. It'll have to be an emergency section." I was pushed through some doors. A doctor was waiting. "O.K." she said to the nurse, "are we ready?" She had the scalpel to my stomach. "No," cried the anaesthetist, "she's not out yet." And then I was....

"Wake up, Dorothy, wake up. You have a fine beautiful daughter waiting for you. It's a girl, Dorothy."

"I know," I muttered, "I know it's a girl. Just leave me alone." I was having such a lovely sleep. Mike appeared from I don't know where. We kissed, we hugged, we cried tears of relief and joy. I didn't discover until much later what Mike had had to go through whilst I was in theatre. In his own words, "I came back after lunch, started walking down the corridor to find six people rushing along in my direction with *Dot* on a stretcher. One nurse looked up at me and said "Hello, don't worry, follow us", and that was it. I followed them. A nurse told me to sit down outside the theatre and wait, so I did. She brought me a cup of tea and I sat there thinking. I weighed up the situation, in my own systematic way. As I saw it there were four possible results. At best I'd end up with a wife and a baby, or I could have a wife and no baby; or a baby and no wife; and, at worst, no wife and no baby. They were the worst twenty minutes of my life."

I was wheeled into the maternity ward. This time I was placed in the centre of the ward, in with a cluster of four beds. The other beds were occupied by women who had cots at the bottom of their bed. I had nothing at the bottom of mine. Suddenly, emotion gripped me. For no obvious reason, I just started crying. I wanted my baby. I wanted her at the bottom of my bed. I wanted her and I wanted her now. I'd been given a Polaroid picture of her and was gripping it tightly. "I want to see my baby," I wailed, "I want my baby." Now logically I knew that the best place for her would be in the Special Care Baby Unit, I knew logically that she would not have been able to survive in a cot at the end of my bed. However, I'd flipped. Perhaps it was a reaction from the anaesthetic. Or relief. I don't know. All I knew was that I wanted her.

They decided that they'd take me down to S.C.B.U. straight away. They were marvellous. Into the lift we went, me clutching the photo in one hand and Mike with the other. We went through those familiar doors again, into the "hot-house". Was it really three years ago that we were here with Sam? It seemed like only yesterday. They wheeled me to an incubator and there she was. She was *so* tiny. So absolutely beautiful. Such a tremendous feeling of joy filled me. My *daughter*. The daughter I was going to share everything with. The daughter I was going to go everywhere with. The daughter who was going to cost her Dad an absolute fortune. The daughter who was *so* wanted. And there she was. Oh, Lydia, Lydia. Such a perfect little girl. Her face was so beautiful. Unlike Sam's face, which had been so battered and bruised when he was born, Lydia hadn't a mark on hers, making her look so perfect. She had lots of wires and tubes on her, which I'd expected. Sam had had all those, so I was totally prepared for that. Her hands looked perfect and so did one foot. The other one was covered in bruises. *That* had been the one which had caused all the damage. It was suggested to me by someone in S.C.B.U. that it was the foot that had kicked a hole in the bag causing it to empty in the first place.

How was she? Was she all right? Were her lungs formed? Did she need a ventilator? Was she a virtual repeat of Sam, or what? These were all questions which we needed answering.

She was doing all right, nothing to cause any major concern. She was in an oxygen box, which was not unusual for a 30 weeker. She had a sticker on her incubator which read "minimum handling". My poor Lydia, she'd had so many needles stuck into her that now she had to be handled as little as possible. It was as if she felt that if anyone were to touch her, it would be to hurt her again. Tears sprang to my eyes. "Oh, Lydia, I want to hold you and cuddle you and love you, but I can't, not yet. But I do love you so very much." I reached through one of the port-holes in the incubator to touch her. She recoiled, so did I. "I'm sorry, Lydia. I'm sorry. I'm not going to hurt you. I promise. I just want to love you. You see, you're so very important to me, so very special. I love you."

I was wheeled back to my ward. Mike stayed with me for a while. I think we were both in shock with it all. He went home to look after Sam. We both felt a sort of action replay of Sam's birth was happening, and felt that we would be able to cope with it all once we'd had a decent night's sleep.

The next day was a fairly routine one. I went down to S.C.B.U. to see Lydia. She wasn't doing too badly. Mike came with Sam to see his sister. Sam was far more interested in the incubator than with his sister and found plenty of toys to play with, so he was quite happy. He'd seen me in hospital before when I'd had my Shirodkar Suture and he'd also been attending (and was still) the children's clinic for check-ups associated with his prematurity. So he was not at all in awe of the place as some children are.

On day three, Lydia came out of the oxygen box and was placed under lights to help with her jaundice. This did not worry us unduly as Sam, too, had had to have the same treatment.

On day four I was allowed to give her a wash and change her nappy. That was at 11.00 in the morning. I had to do it all through reaching through the portholes of the incubator, which was a bit difficult. It was sheer joy to touch my daughter, wash her face and make her comfortable.

At 5.00 p.m. I was allowed to give her a cuddle. The nurse took her out of the incubator, wrapped her loosely in a blanket, carefully arranged the tubes and wires, and put her in my arms. She was so tiny, so fragile. I was so happy. She was my baby. For the first time I could actually hold my daughter in my arms. It was ecstasy. I was so happy. I had to be very careful of the wires and tubes, but I felt very confident in handling her. How different this was compared to the first time I'd held Sam.

Mike was with me when I held Lydia. He'd held off from making any contact with her at all until now. He'd not even touched her while she'd been in the incubator. He admitted to me a long time later why he held off from forming a bond with Lydia. It all stemmed from Sam's jaundice problem, which had frightened Mike. He'd thought that Sam might not survive and had regretted to a certain extent that he had made a bond with Sam from day one. Thus, he'd instinctively held back from making a bond with Lydia, until he'd feel sure that she would survive. He was waiting for day five, this was only day four. Little did we know then what day five had in store for us.

I couldn't have been like that, but then perhaps that's the difference between an emotional mother and a practical father. I cuddled my daughter ever so gently. She looked so lovely. Yet again, I 'm sure it was to do with the fact that she hadn't got a mark on her face; but there was another fact about Lydia that I was unaware of that deemed her to be so beautiful, but I didn't know about that at the time.

I asked Mike to touch her and he did. He put out his finger and rested it under her tiny hand. Her whole hand didn't cover the end of his finger. "Lydia", he whispered and sighed. They bonded. And the next day, he regretted it bitterly.

On day five, in the afternoon, Mike and Sam came to visit us. I was feeling on top of the world. My milk had come so I was feeling quite proud of myself. Ever since Lydia's arrival, I'd been working away on the old milking machine again. They had an electric one now which was quite an amazing contraption. I really did feel like a mother cow, sitting in the "milk room" with a machine pumping away at my nipples.

I'd just "done" Lydia and had gone back up to ward. Mike and Sam arrived. They came and had a chat with me, then went down to S.C.B.U.

A nurse came to me and asked me to nip down to S.C.B.U. to see a doctor about Lydia. "Was anything the matter?" I asked. She turned away and said she didn't know, but that the doctor hadn't sounded alarmed. Off I went, not too concerned, just slightly puzzled.

I walked into S.C.B.U. Mike looked up and seemed surprised to see me. He walked up to me, "Why are you here? Is anything the matter?"

"No, I don't think so. I've just been asked to come here to see the doctor." I felt quite cheerful, which was surprising because I'd expected it to be a bit of a low day. They do say that day five after birth is usually "blues day."

A male doctor came up to us. "Hello, could I have a word with you about Lydia? Let's go into the little room at the end. Nurse, would you like to play with Sam whilst I'm talking to them please?" Sam wanted to follow us. "He can come with us," I said, " we'll just bring some toys into the room." I grabbed some toys, and the doctor, plus a lady doctor, Mike, Sam, the nurse and I went into the little end room, which had three or four comfy chairs in it and a small table. I sat down next to Mike in the corner, with the doctors sitting opposite and Sam and the nurse playing on the floor in the doorway. I was still naively thinking that everything was fine, not considering for one second that anything could possibly be amiss. Mike felt differently, he knew something was up. It was.

"When Lydia was born," the doctor began, "we thought that perhaps there was something "special" about her. But we weren't sure. Sometimes when a child is premature, they have a slightly different appearance to a baby born at term and it's hard for us to give a definite diagnosis until tests are done. We had some tests done on Lydia and I have to inform you that Lydia is Down's Syndrome."

I gasped and put my hand to my mouth. I looked at Mike. He was stony faced. "Which one is Down's Syndrome," I half babbled, half screamed, "which one is it?" I knew which one it was all right. I just didn't want to believe it. "It's a Mongol isn't it? Lydia's a Mongol isn't she?" I sobbed, "she can't be, she can't be."

Sam was looking at me, "What's the matter, Mummy?" he said, getting up. The nurse was frantically trying to entertain him.

"Nothing, Sam," I tried to sound calm. "It's just the doctor telling me about Lydia. She's...she's poorly." I couldn't believe it. I could *not* believe it. *My* Lydia. Down's Syndrome. A Mongol. Mentally handicapped.

25

Impossible. There must have been a mistake. She didn't *look* Down's Syndrome. She was beautiful. There were no slanting eyes. No, they must have made a mistake. We couldn't have a mentally handicapped daughter, we just couldn't.

Throughout all this, Mike said nothing. He sat there, expressionless. And then he spoke, "I *knew* that there was something wrong with this pregnancy. I felt it all along. We've gone through so much for it - we waited so long, we had Dot have a suture to stop the baby being premature, and now *this*. I just *knew*." He was angry. With me? I didn't know. I felt frightened. My whole world was crumbling around me.

"I don't want her," I cried out, "I don't want her. Take her away. I don't want a mentally handicapped daughter. No." I was absolutely horrified. The doctor just sat there and said nothing. I wonder if you've ever had inexplicable prejudices against any type of person - to do with race, religion, colour, nationality, physical disability, height, intelligence, status, profession, and many more. Well for some reason, and I couldn't possibly have told you why, I had always felt uncomfortable in the presence of mentally handicapped people. I would have crossed the road rather than be put in the position of having to talk to someone like that. There was no rational explanation for it. It was just there, in me. And now I found that my own daughter was mentally handicapped. I felt sick. I felt as if my world had totally and utterly collapsed.

My daughter, the daughter who had meant so much to me, was no more. She had gone. She was dead. I cried. I grieved. I hurt. That wasn't my daughter out there in the incubator. My daughter couldn't possibly be mentally handicapped.

"What are we going to do, Mike?" I asked, as if there were any answers to it. There were no answers, only questions. I felt exhausted. "I want to go home," I wailed. "I want to go home, I don't want to stay here. I want to go home with Mike." I clung to his arm.

"Well," said the doctor, "I'm sure if that's what you really want, it could be arranged."

"I'm not staying here. Get me out of this place. Now!" I virtually screamed at them.

Neither Mike nor I remember much of what followed. Things started to go fuzzy. But I knew that it was to be arranged for me to go home that night. Mike took Sam home and came back for me. Meanwhile, the necessary paperwork was being completed.

That night, I went home. I needed to be with Mike. I could not possibly have faced spending the night in that hospital without him. I'd have gone mad. I didn't necessarily want to talk to him. I just needed him, close to me. I felt I couldn't handle this alone. I needed someone else's help. I remember us sitting on the settee, holding hands tightly saying "We'll be all right, we'll get through it, we'll be O.K." I clung to him in bed. My feelings of being an independent woman disappeared. I felt a helpless female in need of someone to lean on, totally. What were we going to do?

CHAPTER THREE

Rejection

Next morning I went back to the hospital, but I couldn't face the thought of seeing Lydia. There was no point. As far as I was concerned, my daughter was dead. We'd decided the previous night to get her adopted. There are lots of people who are quite happy with Down's Syndrome children. They could have her and look after her. *I* didn't want to. My image of life with a mentally handicapped daughter simply made me shudder.

I'd stopped trying to express my milk. Again, there was no point. I'd just wait for it to dry up. What a waste of time and effort that had been. I had tried for four days to get my milk to come, and then they had told me that my daughter was Down's.

Mike did go down to S.C.B.U. Not that he wanted to, but Sam had left his helicopter there the day before, so Mike went to fetch it. He didn't go and see Lydia. He didn't want to. He walked into S.C.B.U. and looked round for someone. A man had his back to him. "Excuse me," said Mike, "I'm looking for someone in charge. Are you in charge?"

The man turned round with a smile on his face. "Well," he said, "in a way I suppose I am." He was wearing a dog collar. Mike pounced. "You're *just* the person I need to see." And that was how Mike met Idris. The two went into a side-room, and Mike let it all pour out. He said, "Why should this happen to me? What have I done to deserve this? Was God picking on me? Had I offended Him in some way?" He cried and sobbed. He was so sad, so dejected, so devastated. He felt he was a reasonably "good" person. Why did this have to happen to him?

Whilst Mike was talking to Idris, I was settling back into my room. The nurse came in and said "Would you like to see the chaplain?"

28

"Yes," I replied, "I would." I didn't know that he was at that very moment speaking to Mike. She went off to bleep him. Shortly after, Idris and I had a lovely chat. I didn't cry whilst we were talking. I think I'd run out of tears. I just wanted to talk, and talk, and talk.... Idris was a super listener. I explained how much I'd wanted a daughter. How the fact that I'd lost my own mother so young had made Lydia's birth so extra special. How I'd felt I'd missed so much through not having a Mum. I'd always felt a kind of envy towards mothers and daughters when I'd seen them doing "nice" things together, like shopping and going out for lunch. They seemed to have intimate conversations and to share close secrets. I wanted to share these things with my own daughter. I'd expected to have that sort of relationship with Lydia. And now I knew that I wasn't going to. It really hurt. I felt as if I was crying all inside and all my insides were hurting, aching for a lost love. But then I was used to not getting what I wanted, wasn't I? I felt so bitter. I don't think we talked about religion. The subject never came up. I just needed a listening ear.

The next day Mike and I had a meeting in S.C.B.U. with a doctor. We told him that we wanted to put Lydia up for adoption. I went to look at her, but I was seeing a different child now. This wasn't my Lydia, but someone else. This was a mentally handicapped child. It felt so strange standing there, looking at her. If only.....I shrugged my shoulders and thought, "She's Down's and that's all there is to it.

That afternoon, my eldest brother Frank and his wife, Barbara, came to see me. I'd told them on the 'phone the previous day about Lydia and had asked them to visit me - because he was my brother and I wanted my family near me. I needed help and I needed him.

It was like a breath of fresh air, seeing them walk into the room. They weren't doctors or nurses or social workers. They were family. I don't know what they'd felt about coming to the hospital. It must have been awful travelling 20 miles to visit your kid sister, knowing that she didn't want her new baby.

They kissed me and sat down. I spoke first, rather than have them struggle for words. "I'm glad you've come. It's nice to have you here. I'm all right." I paused. "Honest." I took a deep breath. "I'm not going to cry in front of you because I don't think I've got any tears left. I've cried and cried because I've got a daughter that I don't want. And I've - we've decided that we're going to put her up for adoption. There's plenty of

29

people out there willing to adopt mentally handicapped children. We've got Sam to think of. We don't want his life ruined by all this." They didn't say much. After all, there's not much to say. I needed their presence rather than their judgement or words of wisdom. Anyway, what could they have said that would make me feel better?

I took them down to see Lydia. We didn't stay long. There was no point. They both gave me a big hug, and went. They were just what I had needed. They'd said they'd do anything they could to help, which was very nice of them. But they could do nothing. Nobody could.

That evening I was discharged, so it took a lot of pressure off Mike. I was so glad to leave that place. It made me feel ill.

I have a friend, Sue, a social worker, who kindly came round to see us. We needed questions answered. We felt that the hospital staff weren't ready to answer them yet. We had been assigned a social worker, but I hadn't felt able to talk to her. You know how sometimes you meet someone and you just know straight away that the two of you are just not going to be able to communicate, well that's just how I felt about our social worker. She had rubbed me up the wrong way the first time she'd opened her mouth. I can't remember her exact words but they were something on the lines of, "Now I'm your social worker and if you feel like letting off steam about anything to anyone then I'm the person to do it to. You just swear at me if you want to. I don't mind. It's all part of my job." I decided then and there that she was the *last* person I was going to bother to let rip at.

I believe the hospital staff acknowledged that we were going through an initial rejection phase, which was not uncommon, and they didn't want us to set the adoption ball rolling too soon, because any day, our rejection phase could end and we'd want to keep her.

So Sue explained the procedure to us and answered all our questions. It was just what we needed. There is a time, after any trauma, and once the initial shock is over, and the anger and rejection have subsided, when one has a thirst for information. Sue gave it to us. She really was a blessing.

You might think us both totally heartless at this stage, but I don't think we were. You see, we were having to consider very far-reaching issues and their implications. We'd churned the situation over countless times, looking at it from every angle. We were quite exhausted with it all. We'd told Sue that we couldn't cope with a mentally handicapped daughter. We wanted her to be looked after and loved by someone else. And there was Sam to consider. He was three years old. We wanted the best for him. His lifestyle would have to change dramatically if Lydia came home. No, it really was in Lydia's best interests not to live with us.

I did have one fantasy solution to it all. I knew that, with a lot of stimulus, physical and educational, some Down's Syndrome children had made remarkable progress, had even achieved "O" levels. I'd imagined Lydia doing the same. I'd have her home and work with her all day, from morning till night exercising her physically and mentally so that she'd be a real "bright" child. But then my bubble would burst. I had Sam and Mike. I couldn't give Lydia what I wanted to. Sam would need more attention than I could give him if I gave Lydia all the time she required. And what about me and Mike? What about our relationship? What a test. It's the sort of stuff that divorces were made of. Indeed, I knew of one relationship where that did happen. My marriage to Mike was my second attempt at getting it all right. My first marriage had been a disaster. I didn't want another divorce. I wanted to live happily with Mike and share my life with him. I knew that my children would fly the nest once they were old enough. My relationship with Mike was, and had to be, more important than my relationship with my children. I couldn't win. Adoption looked the only way out.

The day after Sue had seen us, I 'phoned the hospital, as I had done every morning, to see how Lydia was. And then a bombshell struck. They said that they thought that Lydia had a heart problem. It was then that a pin burst my enormous bubble of self-pity, my feelings of "Poor old Dot. Isn't life awful to you?" Suddenly, I thought only of Lydia, and she again became a person to me, a daughter, rather than an object.

We went to the hospital. I went straight to the incubator, looked at her and wept. Poor Lydia. My heart really broke in half for her. I do love you, Lydia, I love you so much. Please, God, don't let her have a heart problem. Please let her be all right.

We had read that Down's children often have heart problems, and now it was happening to ours. The doctor explained that they were going to do some tests on her. There would, unfortunately be some delay in getting the results because it was Good Friday and the technicians were on holiday. Holiday? How could anyone possibly be on holiday in a hospital? How could we have to wait so long for the results of the cardiograph?

31

Until the following Tuesday we were told. This was our daughter's life we were talking about...! We felt helpless and frustrated, and angry that there was nothing we could do.

We had a miserable Easter, understandably. For Sam's sake we tried to be cheerful, discovering the art of seeming to be really happy. But underneath it all, we had feelings of fear, despair, frustration, anger, resentment, hopelessness. I'm sure there are many people who have felt much the same way. You almost pride yourself, amaze yourself that you can project such an outward appearance of calm, whilst inside it's sheer torture.

On Tuesday, the results arrived. We were taken into a side room. We were told that Lydia had two holes in her heart. The consultant's opinion was that Lydia had between six and twelve months to live. My head started to spin.

How do you react to that? We'd wanted a daughter, we'd got a daughter. We'd been told she had Down's. We'd rejected her - totally. We'd wanted to get rid of her. We'd wanted her to be put up for adoption. When they'd said that she was ill, we'd swung round to accepting her as our daughter again. Now we were told that she was dying.

I felt sick at heart. And yet, in a way, her dying could be a solution to it all. We could love her and give her our all for her short life, and then "try" and get back to "normal", whatever normal was. But how could I want my daughter to die? Was I *so* selfish, *so* self-centred, *so* evil? I must have been, because those emotions were definitely there. And yet, I'd never considered myself in such terms before. Then again - I'd never been in a situation like this before. It was awful. A nightmare.

The next day when we went in, we struck up a conversation with the doctor who'd originally told us that Lydia was Down's. He said that he'd met cases similar to Lydia's and, given her prematurity and the heart problem, he reckoned that she had weeks to live rather than months.

Thursday 3rd April arrived and it proved to be a memorable day. It started with a visit from Kay, my midwife. She had been seeing me regularly. She was concerned about me. I was having an unpleasant discharge. She reckoned I needed a D & C, whatever that was. She said she'd have a word with my G.P.

We went to a meeting with Professor Hull and our social worker at 12 o'clock. His opinion differed from the others. He felt he could not predict the duration of Lydia's life. "She could die tomorrow, but then again, she might not. She could be a survivor," he said.

Yes, I thought. She's a Priest (my maiden name) and a Houghton. She's of tough stock. She'll not give up without a fight. But my head was pounding. My heart was aching. I couldn't take much more of this.

At 1 o'clock we had arranged for Lydia to be christened. It was either Idris or Matty's (the hospital's Deaconess) suggestion that Lydia should be christened, I can't remember who exactly. We hadn't thought about it before. But it was the obviously the right thing to do. We were both in agreement on this. It was a tremendously emotional time. I was shown the "christening cupboard." It was full of beautiful gowns, so tiny that they'd fit the tiniest of premature babies. I chose a totally white outfit for her. It was a really beautiful dress. I also chose a hand knitted christening shawl. It brought tears to my eyes just looking at them, wondering how many children who'd been christened in them had died, and how many had survived.

I washed and changed Lydia, then dressed her. She looked beautiful. I loved her so much. I wished so much she wasn't Down's. I would look at her, talk to her and love her. She didn't look Down's at all. When I look at her photos even now, there's only one or two where you can see that the eyes are on a slant. Perhaps it was all a mistake.

Mathilda, the Deaconess, arrived to perform the christening. She was called "the angel of the hospital" and one could see why. She glided along the corridors, back straight, with a look of total serenity about her, and she spoke softly and gently. Matty (her nickname) placed a cross on the incubator and proceeded to baptise Lydia. I held Lydia throughout the service and cried all the way through it. I couldn't stop myself. Mike and I were the godparents. We'd not asked anyone else to come. It didn't seem right, somehow, to have someone christened whom you had been told might die tomorrow. Who if she survived, you didn't want - and would be put up for adoption. It hardly seemed to be a social event, did it? Mike was quite touched by the fact that some of the nurses stood round for the christening. They were so busy and yet so thoughtful. We went home.

At 3 o'clock the G.P. arrived on my doorstep and told me that I was to go back to the hospital to have a D & C. Frankly, if he'd told me I had to go and have my right arm chopped off, I'd have gone through with it. I was past caring. As far as I was concerned, they could do whatever they

33

wanted with me. So I went back into hospital that afternoon. I was met by a young trainee nurse. He was a really cheerful man who'd tried hard to keep a smile on his face throughout my time there. "Hello, Mrs. Houghton," he said with a grim smile, "How are you?"

I couldn't think of anything to say. I thought hard for a moment. "Pretty pissed off, actually," I replied with a sigh, but not in a nasty way. It just summed up how I felt. "I bet you are," he replied. That night at 9 o'clock I went to surgery. So ended Thursday 3rd April.

The following morning, I went down to S.C.B.U. There I met another doctor who obviously hadn't read our notes. "Down's Syndrome children often have holes in their hearts," he said, with a big beaming smile. "I know of one child who was premature like Lydia, and lived to the age of fourteen, and she was very happy." I screamed inside. I can't take much more of this, I thought.

At 3 o'clock I was discharged. I couldn't wait to get out of that place. If I saw another doctor who gave me another opinion ....

Mike decided that I shouldn't go in to see Lydia that weekend. He reckoned that I needed a break, a breathing space. He took me to Dovedale, in Derbyshire, on the Sunday for a family day out. I 'phoned the hospital both mornings to check that Lydia was O.K. and felt very guilty when I told them that I wouldn't be in to do Lydia's cares, because I so desperately needed some time away from that place. It was closing in on me and making me feel ill. And yet I wanted to be with Lydia, because I loved her. But I also had Mike and Sam to think about. Life was too complicated for me to cope with.

We had a reasonable time in Dovedale. It was lovely to walk aimlessly through the valley and see Sam enjoying himself. Sam had become very precious to me during this time. I loved him dearly and wanted so much to give him the best in life. As I looked at him splashing away in the puddles, I thought about how his life would change were Lydia to come home. Oh, Lydia, what are we going to do?

Let me explain our feelings as they were at that time. Mike and I loved Lydia. She was our daughter, our responsibility. We wanted to do the best for her. O.K., she was Down's Syndrome. She had two holes in her heart. She could die tomorrow. Yet, she might not die. If the doctors all agreed that Lydia had only a very short time to live, then we could perhaps have her home with us until her death, appreciating that this could cause immeasurable distress to our three-year old son and thus to us.

If she were to live for, say, three or four years, what would we do? Perhaps we would consider adoption, for Sam's sake. Why let him grow up having her there as a large part of his life, knowing that he was going to lose her? That seemed like torture. He'd miss out on so much through having a physically and mentally handicapped sister. We'd have to restrict what we could do with Sam because of his sickly sister. It didn't seem fair to him.

But what if we brought her home with doctors saying she'd got only months, and she didn't die? What then?

It seemed that the easiest solution was to say goodbye to Lydia *now*, walk away from the hospital, go home and grieve and leave any more heartache for some other couple. We couldn't face any more ourselves. Why prolong the agony? Just get it over and done with now and start rebuilding our lives without a daughter. Yes, that was the solution.

But it wasn't.

On Monday I went to see Lydia. On Tuesday I took Sam in to see her, and also my friend Lynn with her three year old daughter. We actually had a "nice" time with Lydia. I didn't have any "heavy" conversations with doctors. I almost felt sane. Sam happily enjoyed playing with the toys and I enjoyed having a friend with me. Lydia lay in her cot - she'd been moved out of her incubator - as motionless as ever. She rarely moved.

That evening at 6 o'clock the 'phone rang. It was the hospital. They wanted us to go down. Lydia was having heart failure. She might not last the night. We arranged baby-sitters and got there as quickly as possible. Mike's parents had been our chief baby-sitters throughout all this. They'd been marvellous. We knew that they too were suffering, but we didn't feel that we could handle their pain as well as our own.

Lydia looked very poorly. There was no colour in her cheeks. We knew that there was a bedroom at the end of the ward in which parents could stay with their child at such times as these. That night, someone else was already in it. All they could offer us was the emergency doctor's room. We accepted it gladly. It was a small, narrow room with a single bed. We wheeled Lydia's cot into it and then we were left with her.

It was most strange to be alone with her. It was the first time she'd been with us with no doctors or nurses around. We'd been told what to

35

expect. She'd turn blue and then she'd recover. It had happened several times that evening. So we sat there. Both of us sat on the bed taking turns to cuddle her. And we waited. It was one of those bizarre situations when you didn't know whether to laugh or cry. Sitting waiting for your daughter to die. And you want her to die. And then again, you don't. It was a relief when the doctors had assured us that she was not suffering. Even though she was going blue, she was not in any pain.

It was amazing how calm we were. Why wasn't I crying? The occasion surely merited it. But I didn't feel the need. I wanted to savour cuddling Lydia. It was so nice to be alone with her and Mike. There was nobody else to intrude on our lives. Ever since I'd walked - no, sorry, been carried into that hospital on a stretcher, I'd felt totally under the authority of doctors and nurses. Now I suddenly felt free of them. There were just the three of us and I was relaxing in their company.

As we talked, we cuddled Lydia. We lay down on the bed together, with her between us. Occasionally, Mike would pace slowly up and down the room. I'd keep on checking that Lydia was still all right. And then it happened, she started to go blue. I didn't know what to do, I panicked. "Mike help me, she's going blue." I rocked her frantically, "Please don't die, Lydia, please don't die." And I didn't want her to. I hugged her closer to me, kissing her. "Please, Lydia, I love you, don't die, don't die." Mike had his arms around me, hugging me. We both cried. What a nightmare. Then I looked at Lydia, whose face had gone a pale pink. She was still alive, I felt so relieved. "She's all right, Mike. She's not dead."

After we'd calmed down, we talked about the irony of it all. Here we were waiting for her to die, seeing her death as an answer to all our problems. And yet, when actually faced with her death, we'd not wanted it.

Mike took Lydia from me and cuddled her. "Oh, Lydia," he whimpered, tears rolling down his cheeks, "What are you doing to us? Our lives were so normal, so organised, so predictable, until you came along. You shouldn't even be born yet. You're only three weeks old and you've caused so much heartache and trouble for us. What are we going to do with you? I love you, you know. Do you know that? Oh, Lydia."

I took her back from him. It all felt so weird now, having seen death so close. I'd seen a dead body before - my Dad's - but I certainly had never thought I'd be holding my daughter like this, waiting for her death. We were drained.

36

Twice more that night Lydia turned blue. Both times we held her closely and rocked her. Both times she pulled through.

In the morning a nurse came in to see us. She was amazed to see that Lydia was still alive. So were we. But then we knew that she was a Priest and a Houghton! Idris came to see us that morning. He'd heard that Lydia had been critical. It was nice to see him. Unlike doctors and nurses he was human! He was amazed and delighted that Lydia was still alive. I later learned that sick babies are prayed for in the chapel every day.

At 10.30 a.m. we went home. Lydia was "steady" so we felt safe to do so. We had a quiet day.

The next day Sam had an invitation to a birthday party. I had mixed feelings about going and putting a damper on the party. However, Sam wanted to go, and so I went for his sake. My friend, Julie, was marvellous. It was *so* nice to talk to her. "Hello Dot," she said, "How are you feeling right *now*?" She waited. I knew I could have been totally honest with her. So many people had asked me how I was, but the last thing they wanted to hear was anything upsetting, albeit the truth.

Sam had a lovely time. Goodness knows what was going on in his mind at this time. He was not yet three and I was aware that all this could be doing a lot of damage to him. But there was nothing I could do other than give him as much attention as possible, whilst knowing that, a lot of the time, my thoughts were with Lydia.

Next day we went to do Lydia's 5 o'clock cares. She started vomiting. I felt really frightened. I called for a nurse. She tried to reassure me that Lydia was all right. I left her and drove home, wondering if we would be called back that evening. We weren't.

Two days later, on Sunday 13th April, I went to do her 5 o'clock cares again. Lydia was very poorly. She was very pale. Whilst I was seeing to her, she went blue. I called for a nurse. She grabbed hold of Lydia and dashed her into the "hot room" for some oxygen. I raced after her, trying to fight back the tears. She came round again. I stayed in the "hot room" with Lydia. I sat down on a chair and rocked her and cried and wailed. I felt so raw, so open, I couldn't take much more of this. I couldn't keep up this image of being able to cope and putting on a brave face any more.

"Please, God," I wailed, "just let her die." The nurses in the room looked up at me, shock written all over their faces. Until now I'd felt no judgement from any of them. They'd been well and truly professional in their approach. But now I'd taken them by surprise. I'd taken myself by surprise! I was past caring. I *did* want her to die. I wanted to get it all over and done with. I'd had enough. I wanted to get out of that hospital and run as fast as I could away from it all. I couldn't watch Lydia keep going blue. Was I expected to have fourteen years of this? I couldn't bear the thought of it. No. That's enough.

I eventually went back to the "cool room", where other mothers had seen it all happening. One visiting Grandma came up to me and put her arm round me. "She'll be all right, you know. I'm sure. The doctors and nurses are marvellous here. They can really work miracles. I'm sure she'll soon recover and you'll be taking her home." Inside, I screamed, but thanked her politely. I could hardly tell her that my daughter was dying and that was what I wanted because she was mentally handicapped. That, if she were to recover, we'd be having her adopted, because I couldn't cope with having a mentally handicapped daughter. Well, I could have done, but chose not to. So I said nothing.

CHAPTER FOUR

Acceptance

Lydia looked awful, I didn't want to leave her. I 'phoned Mike and told him what had happened. We agreed that I would stay the night.

The nurses tried to find a nightie for me. All they could find was one of those awful gowns that I'd had to wear when I'd gone to surgery the previous week. I put it on, and we all had a laugh. It's amazing how one can still find the energy to laugh even at such a traumatic time.

The parents' room was vacant. I wheeled Lydia in late that evening, having spent the rest of the time in the "cool room" with the nurses. Lydia had turned blue once more that evening and had taken quite some time to recover. I was now alone with her in a *real* room with a double bed, a bedside table and lamp, a kettle, cups and saucers, a wardrobe, a wash-basin. It was lovely. I got ready for bed and lay down with Lydia nestling between my breasts. I don't know how long we lay like that. Hours probably. I had such a lovely time. I talked and talked to her. About Mike, Sam, the house, where we lived. About the bedroom she would have had. About what we'd have done if she'd lived. About my family and Mike's family. She went blue more frequently now, but I felt more in control of my emotions. I simply left her, between my breasts, stroked and cuddled her, and tried to give her all the love I had intended to give her in her lifetime, all crammed into one night. She didn't stir much, she was too weak.

At about four o'clock in the morning I felt I was going to go to sleep and was scared I might roll over and crush her. So I picked her up, kissed her and carefully put her in her cot. "It's all right, Lydia, you can die now. You'll be all right. I love you."

I woke up about seven o'clock and leaped out of bed. I looked at what I expected to be my daughter's corpse. But she was still alive. I

39

couldn't believe it, nor could the nurses or doctors. I knew that premature babies in Third World countries had survived by being strapped to their mother's bosoms. So I deduced that my cuddles had helped her survive the night.

I'm now going to confess something that might horrify certain readers, but I feel I need to write it down. A nurse had told us, that if we didn't want Lydia to survive a heart attack then all we "needed" to do was nothing at all. Just leave her. Don't resuscitate her. Mike and I in our honest open discussions about Lydia, had spoken of ways we could end the sordid mess we were in. I hasten to emphasise *spoken*. I also emphasise that we did nothing to shorten Lydia's life, as God is my witness, and He most certainly is.

When Mike, Lydia and I had been alone in that doctor's room, Mike had commented on how easy it could have been to have put a pillow over Lydia and suffocate her. He said it, but he wouldn't have done it. But, he said it. We had discussed at some time, the possibility of Lydia coming home with us. "If it ever became too much for us to cope with," said Mike, "I could see me contemplating going into her room one night, putting a pillow over her and suffocating her. I could. For our sakes, and for Sam's. No questions would be asked, I'm sure. They'd say she had just had a massive heart attack, which was expected. Or, perhaps they'd guess the truth but not say anything." He said it, but he wouldn't have been able to do it. When you're desperate, you're amazed at what wicked thoughts can come to mind.

The night I had been alone with Lydia, she had started to turn blue. "I'll do it," I thought, "I'll do it for us." I laid her down next to me and watched her going a deeper shade of blue. Just for a second or two. They seemed very long seconds. And then I snatched her up and held her to my breast, and kissed her and cuddled her and rocked her back to normal colour. How could I have done it? "I'm her mother and I love her." So many thoughts were flashing through my mind. I loved her so much. I now seemed to love her more, as if I'd gone through an emotional barrier, as if all my doubts about accepting her had been dissolved. I was so very happy to be with my daughter. Alone, with no doctors or nurses around watching me.

That's why I'd been so at peace with myself when I'd put her into her cot at 4.00 a.m. She was my mentally handicapped daughter and I loved her so much. I had the power to end her life but I had chosen not to. I didn't want her to die.

I rang Mike to tell him that Lydia was still alive. He came to fetch me, with Sam at about 10.00 am. I could overhear Mike and the staff talking. "We were amazed she survived the night, she was so weak."

"Nothing surprises me any more about this whole business," said Mike with a wry smile. "I've given up trying to make any sense about it all. I've got doctors telling me she's going to die any day, other doctors telling me she could live fourteen years, Professor Hull saying she might not die at all. Last night she looked as if that was it, and here she is today - alive. God knows what today's going to bring." As it happened, nothing.

The next day my twin sister, Margaret, came for the day. She lived in Manchester. It was really nice to see her. We'd talked on the 'phone, but that's not the same as actually being together. Margaret and I are very close nowadays. When we were very young, we'd been very much like chalk and cheese. She was the blue eyed blonde with my mother's characteristics. I was the brown eyed red head with my father's fiery temper. Margaret had always had a calming effect on my Dad. She was the only one who could show and give him the affection that he needed without challenging his authority. I simply challenged him - fullstop. When I think back now at the hard time I gave him, I could cry. Our father died when we were 16. When we were seventeen Margaret went to live with my Mum's sister and her husband, just outside Manchester, and at 18 I went to teacher training college in Birmingham. We saw each other only at Christmas and occasionally at birthdays. Yet we were emotionally close. It was just that our upbringing had led us to live independent lives, not putting on each other. We accepted it as the norm.

Margaret got married and divorced, so did I. Then, somehow we grew a lot closer to each other. We consciously made more effort to see each other and it was good therapy for us both. We liked to talk about the family. I think it was because it had almost been a taboo subject whilst we were growing up. It felt good to talk about problems, emotions, relationships within our family. We would talk for hours about our past. We would try to psycho-analyse all the family and suss out why we were all like we were.

I took Margaret to be with Lydia. We had a lovely time together with her. Lydia was very passive throughout it all. She made so little response to anything. Margaret enjoyed cuddling her and, mercifully, Lydia did not turn blue at all whilst she was there. We spent most of the afternoon there. When we finally came out of the hospital and I drove home, I told Margaret that I felt like two people, living two separate lives. Whilst I was in the hospital I felt that I was Lydia's mother and I could quite happily look after her and care for her. But whenever I left the warmth of the hospital and came out into the cold, sharp spring air, I became Mike's wife and Sam's Mum, with all the responsibilities which that entailed. I just couldn't see how the two me's could coexist. It seemed impossible.

The following day I went in for an hour in the evening, once I'd put Sam to bed. I was trying to give Sam as "normal" a life as possible. Perhaps I shouldn't have. Perhaps I should have let him see me cry. I hadn't had time to read any psychology books on it all.

That evening I went out for a drink with some girl friends, the girls I'd lived with back in 1976. They were so good to me. They let me talk about my situation as much as I wanted, which was a lot.

The next day I took Sam and Mercia, Mike's Mum, to see Lydia. We had a pleasant couple of hours there. Lydia seemed to be going through a reasonably good patch, with no going blue. Sam happily played with the toys. Mercia cuddled her granddaughter. Poor Mercia, fancy her having a mentally handicapped granddaughter. As if she hadn't gone through enough already. She'd lost one daughter in a car crash, when only eighteen years old. It had taken her years to get over it.

Mike came home at tea-time with an enormous basket of flowers from his workmates from B.P.B. Instruments in East Leake, a village some eight miles away from Ruddington. There were chocolates as well for Mike and me and a lovely present for Sam. And a card, which read quite simply, "Dot and Mike, from all your friends at B.P.B. We're thinking about you." Mike and I were both overwhelmed by it. It brought tears to my eyes. That made a change from crying over Lydia.

We were getting such a strange mixture of mail at that time. Such as "Congratulations on the birth of your baby daughter" cards, which, to be honest, I felt like tearing up and throwing in the bin. I knew that people had read the bit I had put in the Evening Post - "To Dot and Mike, a daughter, Lydia Ruth, 3lbs 2oz, born 17th March. With sincere gratitude to staff at Q.M.C." Indeed I'd really enjoyed 'phoning people up and surprising them with my news during the first few days after Lydia's birth.

But these cards felt like salt being rubbed into a wound. They showed pictures of beautiful little girls, all dressed in pink and looking so perfect. And I'd read verses such as; "May she fill your lives with joy," or "How wonderful - a daughter." They made me feel ill. I felt at times as if I was going to physically be sick.

But there were the other cards which meant so very much. Those that simply said "You're in our thoughts," or "Thinking of you in your difficult time." They were *so* welcome.

I had one steady visitor throughout it all, Joy Fiske, who lived just round the corner. She had tragically lost her first daughter when only five years and three months old. Joy was marvellous to me. She'd turn up about once a week, just to have a chat. Sometimes she'd come and let me do all the talking, sometimes she would do it all. She seemed to know instinctively whether she needed to talk, or listen or just go. Sometimes I was really pleased to see her. Sometimes I just wanted to be left alone, to feel sorry for myself and think that I was the only person who could possibly feel so much pain. Yet I knew that Joy had had to wait for her daughter to die, just as I was doing. I was really grateful to her for coming to see me. She was so helpful.

Joy impressed me by the way she had come to accept her daughter's tragic death and how well she was now coping with life. She had, since her tragedy, given birth to two more girls. But even she had to admit that she had heaved a huge sigh of relief when they had both passed the age of five years and three months. Joy always had a smile on her face. How could she when her daughter had suddenly become terminally ill, with hardly any warning? What inner strength she had. Would I ever be as strong as her? Would I ever smile again? It didn't seem possible. I hurt too much. The pain and confusion were so intense at times. I felt as if under attack.

That evening Mike and I went together to see Lydia. We discussed Lydia's health with a lady doctor. She said that, in her opinion, Lydia had just months to live and at most five years. These varied opinions were wearing us down. We needed questions answered, but the answers were all so different. And did it really help us sort out what to do about Lydia? If she did have only months to live, I could perhaps have brought her home with me. Mike, however, had reservations about bringing her home simply to die. Until now our house had nothing of Lydia in it. The bedroom was

43

still the junk room. She had not "made her mark" on the house. Mike wondered if, perhaps, it would be best for us all not to have her home. I could see his point.

If, though, she were to live to the age of five, then what would we do? We thought of perhaps having her with foster parents, with us having access to visit whenever we wanted. It all seemed so callous and cold and calculated, but we were fighting for our sanity here.

Friday was uneventful, Lydia was steady.

On Saturday 19th, Mike took his sister, Sal, to see Lydia. I didn't know how she'd react to seeing her. Sal at that time was not a mother, and she was the first adult member of either family to see Lydia without having felt the emotions of motherhood herself. Sal was extremely sympathetic but I don't think she had any real idea about how we felt. It wasn't until life was cruel to her three years later and her premature son died, that she understood what we had gone through. What is it they say? Lightning doesn't strike in the same place twice, but Satan often does.

Going back to Sal's sympathy towards us, I think that it's the same with anyone who has had some crisis in life. People can be very sympathetic, but it's more helpful to talk to someone who's gone through it themselves and who can fully empathise.

On Sunday we had a "family" day together and in the evening I went to see Lydia. She was not having heart attacks now, but she was not putting on any weight. She hardly wanted anything to drink. It was as if she couldn't be bothered. There was talk of force feeding her, but that we knew, would only trigger off her bowel trouble and give her pain. And we didn't want that.

On Monday I took my good friends Annie, Julie and Melva to see Lydia. I wanted them to see her. I showed Lydia to them as a new mother shows any new child to her friends. Goodness knows how they felt. Awkward, perhaps. I didn't ask. I didn't want to know. I simply wanted to share my daughter with them.

Lydia was still taking hardly any food and didn't look well. I told Mike how poorly she looked. He went to see her that evening. Heaven knows how he managed to keep his job going through all this. His firm had been good to him and told him to take off as much time as he needed, whenever appropriate. That meant a lot to us.

The next morning, Tuesday 22nd, Lydia was not very good again. I must have been terribly naive, but no warning bells were sounding. All this talk of Lydia dying...sometime, I'd not really considered it actually happening. I was talking to a nursery nurse about Lydia and she completely amazed me by asking if we'd consider taking Lydia home with us for a few days. How could I possibly do so? Well I knew that she no longer was having any wires in her and she was being fed by bottled milk via a tube through her nose or via a syringe in her mouth. I could manage a syringe, no trouble, but surely I would not be allowed to take her home? What did she mean by it all? Was Lydia getting better? Would I be able to take her for a walk round the village in her pram? I felt quite excited at the thought of having her home with me. But was it practicable? I couldn't wait to get home to 'phone Mike about it all.

Mike was also confused. What was going on? He decided to 'phone our social worker, to arrange a meeting for us with Professor Hull. It was to be at 5.30 p.m.. the following day.

I decided to go down to the hospital again that evening to do Lydia's cares. She hardly drank anything and the nappy was dry - there were no waste fluids because she wasn't taking any.

Next day we saw Professor Hull. He told us that Lydia weighed only 1.175 kilos, 2lbs 9oz. She was losing weight. Her bowels were causing problems. If she ate it hurt her. If she didn't eat then she would starve and die. It was a "Catch 22" situation. In his opinion, Lydia had four weeks to live.

So now it was four weeks, but I think we'd almost given up listening to any experts. We were too drained and tired to listen, to take any more in. Now what did we do - take her home? Leave her? We couldn't decide. Our powers of decision had been gradually worn away over these past five and a half weeks. Was that all it was, five and a half weeks? It seemed like a lifetime. We couldn't decide what to do, so we went home.

That evening I went back to the hospital with two girl friends, Lynn and Alison. They had been so good to us throughout it all. They'd had Sam for us when we wanted to come to hospital. They'd baby-sat. They'd done the washing up. They'd been marvellous. We didn't stay long because, to be quite honest, Lydia looked very poorly and I didn't want Lynn and Alison to be too upset. Crazy, wasn't I? How could I have been thinking of *them* when my daughter was at death's door. It just didn't make sense. But it was there. Was I trying to protect them, knowing that I couldn't do anything to protect Lydia? I don't know. We popped into the local pub for a quickie on the way home, to try and bring us back to the land of the living. Across the other side of the pub was a small group of teachers from my old Comprehensive school, Fairham. I felt that I couldn't go and join them. I felt as if I had a big sticker on my head that said unclean or killjoy. Surely nobody, whilst out trying to enjoy themselves, would want to talk to me. There again, I *could* go across and force them to talk to me and really spoil their evening, because mine was spoiled already. Oh, why was I feeling so bitter towards people? It wasn't their fault and I knew it. I just sometimes wanted to hurt other people because I was hurt myself.

I knew that they knew what I was going through, but I chose to stay with my friends. I was so very touched when Janet Phillips, the deputy head of the school, came across to me and said something like "It's nice to see you out and about when you're going through such a difficult time." Then, somehow, I didn't feel so "unclean".

The next day I went in the morning to do Lydia's cares whilst Mike took time off to look after Sam. That evening, Lynn came and baby-sat for us. We were planning to go out for a drink. Just before we left the 'phone rang. It was the hospital. Lydia was poorly, would we like to go down? We decided that we'd go to the pub for a quick drink before we went to the hospital. To be quite honest we felt like we needed a drink to give us Dutch courage to get through the evening at the hospital. It was always so oppressive in that place. All we ever seemed to do when we were there was to go round in endless circles. We'd always come away confused by doctors' differing opinions as to the longevity of Lydia's life and the questions of adoption. We'd reached the stage of being absolutely mentally worn out.

We went to the pub for a little while and looked at all these people living happy, normal lives - or were they? Then we went to see Lydia.

She was looking very poorly. She had hardly eaten anything again that day. What was I to do? I'd have liked to have stayed with her. But I thought of Mike needing to go to work the next day, and of Sam. I'd arranged for Sam to go and play at my friend Annie's house the following afternoon, so I'd be able to come to hospital then. I didn't feel right at messing them about too much. We stayed quite late, said goodbye to Lydia yet again, not knowing if I'd ever see her alive again and then went home to the family. They needed me, and were not going to die - well not in the immediate future that I knew of, though I was fast learning to expect the unexpected.

Next morning I 'phoned the hospital. She was still alive, thank God. I spent the afternoon and evening with her. By now Lydia had been put into a single side ward. She'd been taken out of the main ward because her heart attacks had been distressing to the other mothers on the ward and to their visitors.

The following day, Saturday, I didn't go in. I had a day off. I did need that day to be free, not so much from Lydia, but from the building, the nurses and doctors, and the smell of S.C.B.U. I needed to recharge my batteries. That's not to say that I didn't think about her. Of course I did. She was my daughter. I loved her. I 'phoned throughout the day. She was still very poorly but stable. The next day, Sunday 27th, was to be her last.

CHAPTER FIVE

At Peace at Last

I 'phoned in the morning. She was poorly. I said I'd be going in that afternoon. I'd arranged for my brother John and his family to come and see her. They lived at Old Church Warsop, 20 miles away.

I went in and received a shock. I looked at her and knew she was dying. My Lydia was dying. I picked her up. I wasn't going to let her go. Not now. I was going to hold onto her until I couldn't hold her any more. The staff nurse came up to me. She told me she'd been giving her lots of cuddles that morning. She'd been very concerned for Lydia. I'd specifically asked that Lydia should not die alone. I'd asked them to make sure that she died in someone's arms and not alone in her cot. I was so eternally grateful that she'd not yet died and that I could be with her from now on.

I'd arranged to meet my brother in the hospital foyer at 3.00 p.m.. The rules were that no child was allowed out of S.C.B.U. and I certainly was not going to leave her now. Blow the rules. I told the nurse that I had to go to the foyer and that I'd be straight back. She looked at me in despair and then told me to go. I went.

There was almost a sense of "Come on, Lydia, let's show 'em. No hospital rules are going to keep us apart" as I walked along the corridors. My poor Lydia, I thought. You're dying and you've never even seen daylight. All you've known is the bright lights of S.C.B.U. You've never even felt fresh air on your face. It just doesn't seem fair.

My brother was there. We all dashed back to S.C.B.U. - his wife, mother-in-law and two children. The staff nurse was most relieved to see us.

I let them all give her a cuddle, whilst all the time thinking, "Please, God, don't let her die in their arms, please. I want her to die in *my* arms, please, God." They didn't stay long. John could see that I was "distressed"

48

and could see how poorly Lydia was. I was pleased that they'd seen her and they'd met her. But I was pleased when they went, so that I could be alone with her. I wanted her all to myself. I felt that I could ask for that now. Up until then I'd felt I had to share her, I don't know why. But it was different now. This was her last day.

I 'phoned Mike to come down. "She's dying Mike, I just know she's dying, come quickly." He 'phoned his parents.

How did I know? Did I have some in-built system? Was it my mother's instinct? Call it what you will, but I knew. She wasn't bothered about food. I'd tried her with some on a spoon, but she just wasn't interested.

And then she started wailing. I'd never heard it before. She was in pain. She was hurting. I bit my lip hard. No, Lydia, you mustn't be in pain. You can't. You can't start suffering, not now. I took her to the doctor. He explained to me that it was probably her insides starting to fail. Her heart and bowel problems were causing breakdowns within her tiny frame.

It's difficult to find words to express my feelings at that time. I felt overwhelmingly distressed that my little girl, who had done no harm to anyone, was in pain. That her tiny body was suffering. Life was just too cruel. It wasn't fair. I hugged her tightly to me.

Mike arrived and, having looked at her, knew that it was for real this time. No more false alarms. This was it. We went into Lydia's side room. It was very cramped in there. So we were allowed to use the room at the end, the one in which we'd been originally told of Lydia's condition. We wheeled her cot into it.

The doctor came in. "Please," I begged him, "Please, Lydia's in pain. I know we always said that we wouldn't give her anything because all she was having were heart attacks, which didn't give her pain. But she's in pain today. She needs something. We can't let her suffer." He looked at us. He knew that she was pretty weak, yet also that any pain-killer at this stage could shorten her life even more. Then she wailed. "Yes," he said. "She is obviously in pain now. We did say that if she was in pain we'd give her something for it. Just one minute."

He left us alone in the room. I felt in my heart that I was almost signing her death warrant. But I couldn't bear to see her in pain. I didn't want her to die either. But here she was with death written all over her pale, almost grey face. I clung on to her. Mike had his arm around my

49

shoulder. I felt as if we were all part of one body. If Mike had let go, part of me would have packed in working, and we both had to cling onto Lydia to help her through all this pain, to keep her going until the doctor came back.

He gave her an injection. I whispered "thank you" to him and he left us alone. Matty arrived. We'd asked for Idris to come but he was at another hospital. Matty was on call today. She sat and prayed with us. She held Mike's hand and my hand very gently, but firmly. I clung onto Mike's hand so tightly. I needed his strength to keep me going. Lydia was lying on my lap, peacefully for the moment. Her wailing had stopped. She had of course, been drugged. Matty asked God to bless Lydia and to take care of her for us, and to love her for us. Tears were pouring down my face, and Mike's. Oh Lydia, Lydia. The pain inside me was so much. I felt so much despair. Why did all this have to happen? Why couldn't we have had a normal little girl who was coming home with us instead of this awful heartache?

Matty wiped the tears from her eyes and left. We were alone again.

Mike took Lydia from me. "Oh, Lydia, why have you done this to me?" he sobbed to her. "I wasn't going to get close to you and now look what you've made me do." He held her closely to him and rocked her. She was totally impassive now. She was grey, no movement at all. No reaction to being touched. I was so pleased to see Mike with her like that. It was so necessary for him, so vitally important to be 100% in love with her and .... at peace, I suppose is the word I'm searching for. He had now totally accepted that he was Lydia's Dad, whether he wanted it or not, and he was in love with her. It was a beautiful moment for us all. And so necessary for part of the healing process. God knows what he'd have been like if he'd still held her at arms length, figuratively speaking, and she'd died. In mental torment I suppose.

We sat with her, taking turns to cuddle her. We were brought some sandwiches. I couldn't eat, Mike managed a bit - I wondered how he could. I changed her nappy. She looked all skin and bones and made no movement. She just lay there. Her nappy was clean. Of course it would be, she wasn't eating or drinking anything. We were playing a waiting game.... sitting and waiting for her to die. We knew it was going to happen. It's strange that, once you've accepted that it's inevitable, you become emotionally resigned and say "Come on, there's nothing else you can do now. You'll cope." And you do.

I was holding Lydia. She seemed to be losing whatever natural colour was left in her. Throughout the greyness of her complexion, there had still been a very faint, but life-like tinge of pale pink. But it had now gone.

"Mike," I said, alarmed, "I think she's gone." He clung onto me and Lydia. And she had. No wail. No look of pain. No anguish. She had simply stopped breathing. We sat there, stunned. So that was what it was like to see someone die, was it? I sighed. It was almost a sigh of relief. She'd gone so peacefully. Thank you, God. So that was it, was it? Lydia gone. We sat there for some time in silence.

Mike blew his nose. "I'll go and tell someone," he said. He left me alone with her and came back with a staff-nurse and a doctor. A new doctor. I'd never seen him before. He gently took Lydia from me. He unwrapped her and placed his stethoscope over her heart. It went through my mind, "He's going to tell me that's she's not dead. That she's fine. That she'll be all right." He looked up at us, "I'm sorry, she's gone." I bit my bottom lip and set my chin firm. "Thank you," I smiled. It was as if I had to put on a brave face for *his* sake. I must have been mad!

He left us. The staff-nurse stayed. We knew this one pretty well. She'd been very kind to us. "I'll leave you alone with her for a while," she said. She left us. Mike looked at his watch. It was 7.15 p.m..

I don't know how long we sat there with Lydia. Time was standing still. Time was of no importance. I cuddled her. Mike cuddled her. We didn't cry. We were too worn out to cry. It was nice cuddling her.

Some time later, the staff-nurse popped her head round the door. "Can I come in?"

"Yes, sure."

"I thought you'd probably had enough time alone with her by now."

Matty reappeared. She'd been contacted at home and had come back. That was nice of her, I thought. She said prayers again for Lydia, and for us. She thanked God that Lydia was now at peace and asked Him to look after her for us. "Yes, God, she's far better off with You than she would have been with us," I thought. The prayers made us all cry. Matty left.

The sister took us under her wing. "Would you like to come with me, Mum, and help me choose some pretty clothes for Lydia ?"

51

I gently put Lydia back into her cot. The nurse took me to another cupboard in which there were lots of plain, simple dresses and outfits for laying babies out in. It touched my already exhausted heart. I chose a lovely white dress with pale pink embroidery for her.

"That's a nice one. She'll look lovely in that," smiled the sister. We walked back into "our room". "Now, I suggest that the two of you disappear for an hour. Go and get some fresh air. Go for a walk, or a bite to eat, or go to the pub. Yes, that's it, go to the pub and get a drink. I bet you could both do with one right now. Have a good stiff drink, and when you come back Lydia will be all spruced up for you and looking beautiful."

Now to some people, that could have been totally the wrong thing to suggest. But, do you know, to us it was exactly the *right* suggestion at that time. I *did* need a drink. I *did* need to get out of that place and breathe some fresh air. She was *so* right. And that's just what we did. We walked out of the hospital with me clutching Lydia's white, cuddly rabbit that our good friends Jackie and Mick had sent to her. I had to cuddle something. I couldn't cuddle Lydia any more and my arms felt so empty. I also held on to Mike so tightly. I did so need him. We went to a pub next to the hospital. I had a double brandy whilst holding onto my rabbit. I looked around at all the people there, laughing, enjoying themselves. It all seemed so dream-like. Was I really in a pub, having a drink, while my daughter was lying dead in a hospital? Mike and I both mused over it all. It all seemed so bizarre.

We went back an hour later. Lydia was changed and was no longer in a cot. She was in a Moses basket. The sister greeted us with a beaming smile. "I'll leave you alone with her."

We sat with her for I don't know how long. Eventually we went out to look for our sister. "We've said our goodbyes to her. What's going to happen to Lydia now?"

"Well, she'll be taken down to the Chapel of Rest, where she'll stay the night, and then she'll be taken to Lymm's, the funeral directors in town. All the arrangements for her funeral will be completed by the hospital, and all the costs, too, so you needn't worry about the finance side of it."

My eyes opened wide in amazement. I hadn't even thought about funerals, let alone any costs. It hadn't even entered my head that money had to be considered when talking about Lydia. It seemed a sordid word. How could anyone talk about money at such a time? But, of course, I wasn't being realistic. Again. "Who will take Lydia down to the Chapel of Rest?" I asked.

"Well, usually it's the night porter"

"Could we go with him, please? I'd like to know where she is, if you don't mind." Until now, we'd always known exactly where Lydia was - S.C.B.U. The thought of going home and not being able to picture where she actually was made me feel uneasy and unhappy.

The sister smiled at me, "Well, it's not been done before, but I don't see why you shouldn't go with her. I'll come with you as well if that's O.K. You never know, you might be setting a precedent here."

So we all went to the Chapel of Rest. It was strange, going along the very quiet corridors, carrying a corpse. I didn't know what to expect to find in the Chapel. I'd never thought about what one would look like before. I'd never been in this situation before. We walked into the Chapel and I was immediately aware of a great and wonderful feeling of peace. I didn't feel as if I was in a hospital. It didn't have any of the hospital smells. It was different here. Lydia would be all right here. I felt all right now. The porter waited outside. We only stayed a minute. We just wanted to know where she was. The porter escorted us back to S.C.B.U. The sister started talking fairly cheerfully to us again. "Some of the other staff thought I was awful suggesting that you should go to the pub. Did you?"

"Oh, no," we both agreed, "it was just what we needed." We said our goodbyes to the sister and thanked her for her help. She beamed at us and gave us both a hug. She'd made it so much easier for us. A real Godsend. We went home, to Mike's parents, who looked worn out by it all, and to Sam.

There came a period after Lydia's death when we tried to just get on with life. It seemed so strange being at home. I could easily have imagined that this nightmare had never happened. Nothing seemed different in the house. It wasn't as if we'd made Lydia's bedroom ready for her. Perhaps it really hadn't happened. Was it just a bad dream?

Different people's reactions to our situation were interesting to say the least. There are, I'm sure, lots of books which give advice about what to say and what not to say at times such as these. It's often a topic for discussion between friends after a tragedy of some kind. I have to say that

53

I was truly amazed at the comments made by friends and family throughout the whole Lydia saga and beyond. I know that many of them must have really struggled to know what to say. Perhaps the whole subject should be on the National Curriculum to try and bring up a generation who will know how to cope with responding to tragedy. After all, the only certainty in life is death.

I knew I was going to get "Well, she's better off where she is now," and "You didn't want a mentally handicapped daughter, did you?" and "It's a blessing really," and "You can try for another one, you're young enough" and "Time heals." I also got quite used to people trying to avoid the subject. "Don't talk about it. Act as if it never happened." "Did you know, she's got a photograph of Lydia on her mantelpiece?" Someone told me to take it down and tuck it in a drawer out of the way. I became quite used to seeing people hurrying past on the other side of the street with their own little girls, sometimes acknowledging me with a look that seemed to me say "I don't want to have to talk to her because it depresses me". Or people actually crossing the road to the other side. Or the 'phone ringing and the caller not bringing the subject up - as if it could possibly *not* be on my mind. I became quite good at putting on a "brave face" and saying I was O.K. rather than embarrass them, or have them struggling for words. There were very few people with whom I could really be myself. There just didn't seem to be any point in talking about my innermost feelings with someone who couldn't possibly understand or cope with the torture going on inside me.

Please don't misunderstand me. I had some super friends who I knew really wanted to help me. It must have been so very frustrating for them. But they hadn't gone through what I had and couldn't possibly relate to me. They could sympathise, but not empathise. In a situation like that, you need empathy.

I could talk to Mercia about the loss of a daughter, and to Joy, who had watched her daughter die. I eventually came across a couple who had rejected their child. A friend had had post natal depression, she was a great help. My friends tried so hard to help me. But I felt so alone in it all. I kept crying for my Mum in all this. I needed my Mum. But I hadn't got her. Goodness knows how she could have helped me. But I just felt she'd have known what to say and do.

On Tuesday, I had to go for my six week post-natal to the Q.M.C. Imagine my horror when I discovered that I had to sit in the same queue as women waiting for their antenatals - the same women I had seen at my previous antenatals. Talk about torture! Did they have to be so happy?

I went in to see the doctor. A nurse came to get me ready for him. She smiled at me - "And how's baby?"

I couldn't stand it and burst into tears, "She died on Sunday."

The nurse's face fell. "I'm so sorry. I'd no idea. It's not on your records. What happened?"

"She was ten weeks premature. Down's Syndrome. She had two holes in her heart and died of a heart attack." I blurted out. That summed it up pretty neatly.

"I'll go and tell the doctor." She hurried out. He walked in a few minutes later and was really kind to me. He gently examined me and said that, physically, I looked quite well. I asked him, out of curiosity, to establish whether I'd had my 16 week blood check for abnormalities. I doubted whether it had been carried out. He went out and came back later looking very angry. "No, it wasn't done. I can only apologise."

"It doesn't matter," I said, "I just wanted to know, that's all." A friend of mine suggested that I should sue the hospital for thousands. You see, although the 16 week test is primarily for detecting a Spina Bifida baby, it could perhaps have detected some other abnormality. But I wasn't interested in revenge. So what if I'd got thousands? It wouldn't have bought me another daughter. I was too emotionally upset to volunteer for extra stress.

The next day Mike and I went to see Lydia at Lymm's, the funeral directors. They were near to the city centre. We'd wanted to see her the day she'd been transferred there from the Chapel of Rest, but we'd been told we'd have to wait until Wednesday at the very earliest. The funeral was to be on the Friday, and people didn't usually go to "view" until the day before a funeral.

We were pleased to see her again. It had troubled me not knowing what the funeral parlour was like. It didn't seem right. I needed to have a picture of her, and where she was, in my mind's eye. It gave me peace.

The day of the funeral came. It was to be at 9.15 am., which pleased us. We had a "get it over and done with as soon as possible" feeling about it. Sam went to a friend's. We'd gone through all the kid-ology of whether he should be there, but decided that he was too young and he might stop adults from doing whatever they wanted to do naturally. I didn't want to have to put on a brave face yet again, this time for Sam's sake. It was bad enough with non-family, and family, come to think of it.

I did make sure to take Sam to the crematorium later, when he was about six years old. I didn't want him to end up like me. My Dad had decided not to let Margaret and myself go to Mum's funeral. We were four years and eleven months old at the time. We were not included in any of the paraphernalia of the funeral. We were shielded from it all, kept well away. So much so, that there were times when, as a little girl, I used to imagine that perhaps she hadn't actually died. Perhaps she'd just had enough of us and had walked out. Perhaps one day she'd come home. There were times when I'd hear the back door open and I'd wonder if it was my Mummy. I'd wonder if I'd perhaps been instrumental in her leaving us all. Perhaps I'd been so naughty that she'd had enough of me.

Dad wouldn't let us go to the cemetery. Why, I wondered? He reckoned that there was no point in going there. He'd had no gravestone erected. He never went there to take her flowers." A waste of money. Why spend money on the dead? Spend your money on them when they're alive, not when they're dead. Once they're dead they don't need any money." That was his philosophy. And I have to confess that to a degree I agree with him. But not being able to see her grave made me unable to acknowledge her death. Hence my dream of seeing her walk through the door.

It was not until I was ten or eleven that I saw her grave. Margaret and I decided that we wanted to go and find it. So one Sunday afternoon, we walked to the cemetery. It wasn't that far - about fifteen minutes walk from our house. This was, of course, in the days when it appeared quite safe to be allowed to roam. Our housekeeper, Mrs Drury, had told us where the grave was. It had only a rosebowl. So off we went.

Once in the cemetery we realised that we were looking for a needle in a haystack. So many graves. So many rosebowls. It seemed an impossible task. We searched for ages. Then suddenly my brother, John, appeared. He was visiting his girlfriend. Her parents' bungalow looked out over the cemetery, and they'd seen us. He'd come to find out what we were doing. We told him. He took us to the other side of the cemetery. We'd never have found the grave without him. Then he left us. I gazed at the grave in awe. Was this actually where my Mummy was? Were the remains of her body under this mound of earth? Was she really here? We sat there and didn't say much. It was then that I could finally let her be dead and buried. Afterwards, I would quite regularly go down to see her. I'd take the garden shears with me and tidy up her grave. And I'd talk to her. Lots. It was very therapeutic for me, because I felt that she was listening to me, because she was right next to me. Nowadays, of course, I don't do that. Indeed I know that it's futile to do so. I've changed.

For Lydia we had a very small funeral. Immediate family only. No flowers. We asked for donations to be sent to S.C.B.U. Mike and I had a small floral cross to put on top of the coffin, but that was all. I'm afraid I've always been against sending a lot of flowers or wreaths at funerals. To me it only lines the pockets of the florists. I'd far rather send the money to a charity. Don't get me wrong. I've often gone to the Crematorium and spent time looking at the beautiful wreaths which have been left from a recent funeral. I've truly admired their beauty, and I'm sure that giving something beautiful as a last gift must be a great comfort to bereaved loved ones. But my upbringing has made me a very practical person, and that's the way I am.

Idris performed the service for us. It was good to see him again. He said some very comforting words for us. I liked him.

That evening I took Sam to the doctor because he'd got spots. It was German Measles. Poor old Sam. Well at least he could get some undivided attention again. Thank God he'd not been ill while Lydia was alive.

57

CHAPTER SIX

Your Daughter's not in Heaven

Life carried on. My friends were very good to us. They rang. They invited me and Sam round. They listened to me. They sympathised with me. They let me cry. They did everything they could to help me. I saw the doctor, and he too was very sympathetic. And yet I just hurt inside, and nothing anybody said could take it away. It felt like there was a knife cutting away in my heart. It hurt so much. There were days when I literally wanted to curl up and die.

And yet I had Mike and Sam. And I loved them. Heaven knows how I'd have been if I'd not had Sam to look after. I had to keep going for his sake. At times, though, I didn't want to go on. I'd had enough. I felt so confused and at a loss. What was I going to do?

Mike and I decided that we'd move house. We'd originally said that we'd do so, probably when the baby was a year old. (Why do we make plans?) A move would occupy our minds. I know that one is not supposed to move house when one has just lost a loved one. It's in all the books. But we'd made up our minds and that was that. We sold the house very quickly. We'd had no doubts that we'd sell it without difficulty. We looked at houses in the neighbouring village of Keyworth, and in Ruddington and found just what we were looking for in Ruddington. I was pleased. For the same price, Keyworth houses were bigger than those in Ruddington, but there was something special about this one in "Rudd". They say it's like when you fall in love - you just know when it's the right one. And I knew it when we saw it for the first time. It all happened quickly and fairly smoothly. From putting our house on the market to moving into our new home took three months.

So, on August 22nd 1986 we moved to our new house in Ruddington. During those three months my friends were so good to me. I really can't stress that enough. They helped me as much as they could and I shall be eternally grateful to them.

We managed a holiday. We went to the New Forest in the south of England for a week and had a relaxing time there. It was good to be away from everyone. Not having to think of anyone else. I had spent so much time and effort trying to comfort others who seemed to me so inadequate in helping me that I felt exhausted from it. You might say "Then why did you bother seeing people?" But it's so strange. I needed to be with people, to talk to them and cry with them, to lean on them, as indeed they wanted me to. I couldn't have borne being alone in all this. I think I would have cracked up. I felt that, if I burdened them, some of my pain might go from me to them. I didn't want to hurt them, but I was desperate.

In July, we went to the other major hospital in Nottingham, the City Hospital. There we saw a lady from the Clinical Genetic Service. She told us that the blood samples analysed had shown that no hereditary factors were involved in Lydia's Down's Syndrome. The chromosomes had, for some unknown reason, not formed as they should have done. She told us that the chance of us having had a Down's Syndrome baby, given our ages, had been 1 in 850. The chances of it happening again were 1 in 100. That hit hard. Why us? Surely it couldn't happen again? We were assured that it had indeed happened to certain couples. We could not rule out the possibility of it happening to us.

I also saw my gynaecologist from the Queen's in July. She said that, in her opinion, I could consider becoming pregnant again. She had little or no reservation about my physical condition, but didn't touch on my mental state.

At the beginning of August, just before we moved house, we had a French boy to stay with us for two weeks. It was a good distraction for me. He was a paying guest, through an agency. Sam enjoyed his company and so did Mike. They'd disappear in the evenings and go exploring. It did Mike good. He too needed a distraction. He'd gone through so much. Much more than he was admitting.

In the September, I started going to a Swing into Shape class on a Monday night. We'd decided that it would be unwise for me to go back to teaching French at night school. I'd been teaching "Holiday French" or "Beginners French" for several years. It had always been so refreshing for me to take a class of students who were all keen to learn the language,

59

who had indeed paid to learn it. It had given me the strength to battle on with my not-so-keen pupils who I had during the daytime. But....I was still very "up one day and down the next". It would not have been right for me or for the students to try to attempt anything like that just yet.

I'd been so used to being out at least one night of the week. I didn't think I could cope with being in every evening. Yet I didn't want to go to anything that would make a lot of demands on me. I didn't feel that I could cope with any pressure. So off I toddled with my new leotard, determined to try and enjoy myself. I'd never considered myself a Swing into Shape person. What do I mean by that? Well somehow, perhaps through all the jokes that one hears about swing into shape classes, I'd envisaged that the class would be full of women who were bored and boring housewives of limited intelligence, to whom Swing into Shape classes would be really taxing and the highlight of their week. However, I was pleasantly surprised. The 'girls' were a wonderful mixed bunch of pensioners, middle-aged and youngsters, all determined to have a good time. I'm afraid I didn't throw myself into it like the others. I kept myself firmly on the back row and tried to join in and look enthusiastic. But I suppose I was trying for the impossible. My heart wasn't in it. My heart wasn't in anything right now. I must have been a real wet blanket. I'd try and join in the chatter at the coffee break, but I just couldn't laugh like the others. It just didn't sound right. It sort of echoed around me. I knew that I had changed. I was a different person. I used to enjoy a good laugh with a crowd of girls - but now I felt, quite simply, a killjoy. Poor old Dot, and poor old everybody else in the class.

It was in October that I was stopped by a lady who lived in the next street. She thought I was new around the neighbourhood and asked if I would like to pop round one afternoon for a coffee? Little did I know what an impact Sylvia would make on my life.

The year ended quietly, thank goodness. We had a fairly good time, socially. We saw the people we wanted to see and hoped we were not too miserable to be with. Sam, of course, forced us to be reasonably cheerful. Christmas was strange, inasmuch as we'd envisaged it with two children and we only had one. Some people might say "well at least you've got one," and I agree. But we had expected two.

Emotionally, I was still very weepy. I did very little crying in front of Sam. With hindsight, I think that perhaps I should have. I should not have protected him from the realities of life. Was I bringing him up to accept that his sister was dead and Mummy didn't cry? I was becoming just like my Dad! I'd cursed my Dad for not having had a good cry in front of me about my Mum and now I was doing exactly the same to my son. Hypocrite!

I was trying not to be too weepy in front of Mike, but it was difficult. It was as if I'd held on to my emotions all day long, going about my business, taking Sam out to play with friends, having friends around and putting on a brave face; and then, once they'd all gone and Sam was in bed, I'd let it all pour out. It's a wonder Mike didn't walk out on me. I couldn't have blamed him. There he was going out to do a hard day's work at the office, and coming home to a miserable weepy wife who complained that friends weren't being sympathetic enough for her. Just what he needed! I wanted to know what *he* was going to do about all the pain I felt. I really was wrapped up in total self pity. I was a mess. I really missed Lydia, I wanted to be close to her and talk to her. I felt that I couldn't go to the crematorium with Sam and have a good cry - perhaps I should have done. Then I thought of going to the local church if that was all right with Mike. He said he didn't mind. Yes, I'd feel close to her there. So I started going to the evening service. That way it wouldn't interfere with our family day-time together. Mike very obligingly put Sam to bed for me. I can't emphasise enough how wonderful Mike was to me at this time. He was the epitome of a caring husband. He was so kind to me, so unselfish, in spite of what he must have been going through. What a man.

There are three churches in our village, an Anglican, a Baptist and a Methodist. The Anglican one is a fairly big, impressive building right in the middle of the village, whilst the other two are quite modest in size and, to be honest, I hadn't as yet, even noticed them. I considered myself C. of E. so I went to the Anglican church. When I say that I considered myself C. of E. what I mean is that I'd been brought up to believe in God and Jesus and the Bible, I'd not been a member of any specific church, so if I had to label myself with any particular church, I'd have gone for C. of E.

I think it's a lovely building. I felt comfortable and relaxed in it straight away. They do say that finding the right church is like finding the right house or partner. You just know when you've found the right one. It's not too old for me. I don't like the really old ones. They do nothing for me, personally. Not like Mike. He really loves those big, old ones, like York

Minster or Southwell, our local Minster. St. Peter's was built in 1888. There are about twenty rows of pews and a nice wide carpeted aisle leading down to what I later discovered is called the screen. I'd never come across the vocabulary used for the different areas of an Anglican church. I hadn't known that the area where the congregation sat was called the nave, nor that the bit where the choir sat was called the chancel, the two separated by the screen. It amused me that the vicar disappeared behind this screen at certain moments during the service. There must have been some reason for it, but it seemed rather bizarre to me. I mention the screen here because mounted at the top of it is a massive wooden cross. This cross looked so simple among all the richness of the other fittings in the church. I liked it. And it was to become very precious to me later on.

I would go in and sit on the right hand side, at the back. I'd listen sometimes to the vicar, but honestly I hadn't come to be with him, or with anyone else. I just wanted to be with Lydia. I'd go through the service as printed in the books, but very often I'd simply said the words rather than try to understand them. After all, I'd come to be with Lydia. I'd have a good cry, sitting there. Crying made me feel better. It was as if a tiny bit of the pain was forced out of me with those tears. It was good therapy.

Nobody bothered me. I didn't want to be bothered. I wanted to be left alone. With Lydia. And my Mum. And my Dad. I didn't half cry for my Mum. I really wanted her. I really needed her. She'd have understood what I was going through. She'd have helped me. She'd have given me the answers that nobody else seemed able to. Or would she?

It was in that church that I started to openly grieve for my Mum. I realised that I'd never grieved properly for her. My Dad had never grieved for her openly, in front of me, nor had my brothers. So I'd never had a real good sob for her. But I did now. And then there was my Dad. In that church I began to talk to my Dad. And it was in a way that I'd never spoken to him before. In my pain, I somehow felt that I could feel the pain that *he'd* felt when my Mum had died. The absolute anguish he must have felt. The full horror of what my Dad had gone through, to see his wife dying of cancer, in pain, and knowing he'd have five children to bring up by himself, alone, when he was such a proud and independent man. How terrible it must have been for him.

I'd never really grieved for my Dad before. You see, when he died I was nearly 17 and going through a pretty rebellious stage with him. I was sad at the time and did have a good cry, but it was not true grieving. Perhaps I was too young to grieve. Or perhaps I did not want to grieve because, in my heart of hearts, I felt a great sense of relief that this man, who had, in my young eyes, shown me no affection, but had simply disciplined me and fed and watered me, had now gone and I'd now be able to "do my own thing". I really had not felt loved by my Dad at all.

As I went to church each Sunday, I started to think of him in a more grown up way. He must have loved me. I was his daughter. I remember the one and only occasion when I discovered that he really did care for me. My Mum had a sister who lived in Leigh, a town just west of Manchester. We'd often visit her. We loved going to see her. She had no children of her own and she sort of adopted us as her own. I think that Margaret and I considered her as a surrogate mother rather than an aunt. She openly loved us. It was so good to sit next to her and be cuddled. I didn't seem to have cuddles from anyone else.

We used to go and visit her as a family, but one summer she invited just us two girls to stay, to give my Dad a break. Margaret and I leapt at the chance. No Dad to tell us what to do. Great! We'd be about 11 or 12 at the time. Well we went there for about a week and had a "heavenly" time. She pampered us, spoiled us, talked with us, kissed us, cuddled us. I can still remember her goodnight phrase to us. "Goodnight. God bless. Sweet dreams." There was something in what she said that always touched my heart. I use those words nowadays with my children. That week was bliss. We always cried whenever we left her house to go home. This time was no exception.

When we arrived home we walked through the door to be met by my Dad, just sitting in his usual big chair in the kitchen. "Hello," we said. "Huh," he grunted, "so you've decided to come back then, have you?" He stood up and walked away. I walked upstairs with my case. Margaret followed my Dad. "Now, there's no need to talk like that. You knew we were coming home today and we're home now." She was always the calming influence in the house. She'd taken over the role as wife/mother. What a burden.

It was some time later that we discovered that he'd written a letter to my aunt. She showed it to us. It was something along the lines of "I wish you wouldn't take the girls away from me. They're all I've got left to live for. Don't do it again." Even though it was so many years ago, I remember it all so clearly. I was amazed. Was I really loved by my Dad? Did he really care for me? Couldn't he live without me? So in church I cried and cried and cried. And it felt so very good.

As soon as the service finished, I'd nip out quick so that I didn't have to speak to anyone. I didn't want to. Sometimes the vicar might have reached the door and I'd have to shake his hand, but usually I managed to get out without having to do that. I really didn't want to have to be bothered with people. Not here. I'd come here to escape from them.

One Sunday evening in church someone came and sat next to me. She asked if she could join me. Of course, I couldn't refuse. But I couldn't be myself then. I couldn't cry like I wanted to. She was imposing on my airspace. I felt cramped. At the end of the service she introduced herself. She was Gill Harrison, the vicar's wife. Gill would regularly sit with me. She, too, was to make a big impact on my life.

It was a weekday. Sam was at nursery. I was alone in the house. The doorbell rang. I wasn't expecting anyone. I opened the door and there stood two Jehovah's Witnesses whom I knew fairly well. They'd quite frequently appeared on my doorstep at the last house and I'd happily had a chat with them for 5 or 10 minutes about the meaning of life. They'd been happy for me when I told them I was pregnant and had helped me in my grief by actually crossing the road to listen to me pour it out to them. I was grateful to them for listening to me. They never seemed to avoid me, not like I felt some people were doing. To have someone deliberately make the effort to share my sad time was a real boon. To this day I am still very grateful for their concern and support which I so desperately needed.

They asked me how I was and how I was settling into this house. I told them that I was gradually coming to terms with losing Lydia. That at least she wasn't suffering now that she was in Heaven. I knew my Bible well enough to know that in Heaven there is no pain or suffering.

"Your daughter's not in Heaven."

I froze. "Pardon?"

"She's *not* in Heaven." My heart started to beat very fast.

"Of course she's in Heaven." I said, biting my bottom lip. I was trying hard not to sound too upset.

"No," he said, looking at his wife. He rummaged in his bag for his Bible. "Look here," he said, whilst flicking through the well-worn pages. He began to quote me verses from the Bible that sent my head reeling.

64

Lydia? *Not* in Heaven? I couldn't cope with this. But I thought that when you died you went to Heaven. Unless you were a real baddie and then you went to Hell. Lydia couldn't be in Hell. Surely not.

"No," Stuart was saying. "When a person dies they have to wait until Judgement Day, when everyone will be judged. It's only after Judgement Day that the chosen will go to Heaven."

I felt that I'd break down crying if I heard much more of this. I struggled for words. "I......I don't think I can accept what you're saying," I stammered, trying to keep calm.

"Well, it's all here in the Bible."

I politely but hastily said goodbye to them, closed the front door, walked into the lounge and promptly burst into tears. Lydia, Lydia. Of course you were in Heaven. Of course you were. You weren't in some no-man's land. You're there now, with my Mum, in Paradise, with Jesus. And Dad, well I didn't know about my Dad. I was confused about him. I didn't know whether he was a Christian or not. But my Mum was. She'd been a Sunday School teacher years ago. She was definitely in Heaven. I couldn't cope with thinking that Lydia was anywhere else but in Heaven. How could those two J.W.'s hurt me so? How could they do this to me?

I struggled through the rest of the day in a daze. When Mike came home from work he knew immediately that something was wrong. I told him what had happened and he was furious, so angry that they could upset me so much, that they could be so insensitive.

He put his arms around me. "Look," he said, "let's get someone else round to talk to you about it, to calm you down. Let's ask...." he thought for a moment, "the vicar. Yes, the vicar will come and talk to you....to both of us about it all. Will that help?" My lovely Mike, he always knew what to do. He was such a good husband, I didn't deserve him.

The next day I 'phoned the vicar and asked him to come round. I didn't, and indeed couldn't say much on the 'phone. I simply asked him if he would come and talk to me and my husband because we were confused about a few things. I remember that I could hardly speak to him on the 'phone, I was very choked up. When I put the 'phone down I had a good cry. I did so need to know that Lydia was in Heaven. She'd got to be.

He came round a few days later in the evening, once Sam had been tucked up in bed. I quickly told him about Lydia and that we thought she'd gone to Heaven. I told him about the J.W.'s comments and how upset and confused I'd been. That was why we'd asked him round - to end our confusion.

He sat there, listening. When I'd stopped talking he took a deep breath and then said to us: "I want you to know right now that Jesus is looking after Lydia. He is looking after her." I breathed, almost sobbed a big sigh of relief. "Thank You," I thought. "Thank You, God, thank You, Jesus. I could now picture Lydia with Jesus in Heaven. This fuzzy picture that the J.W.'s had given me of her being nowhere in particular disappeared. I felt safe, secure again. I saw Lydia safe in Jesus' arms.

The vicar could go home now, I felt. But he didn't. He went on to explain to us the conflicting verses in the Bible about life after death. I can't remember them exactly, but I do remember him quoting the story of the crucifixion. When Jesus said to one of the robbers "I tell you the truth, today you will be with Me in Paradise." That verse remained with me and comforted me. Lydia. Paradise. Jesus. I could relax now. That throbbing in my head stopped.

When the vicar had finished discussing things with us, he had a cup of coffee with us. I initially asked him if he'd like a beer or a lager, but he declined saying he didn't think that it would be appropriate. I was quite impressed by that comment. You see, the only other vicar I'd known was the one who lived in Church Warsop, where I'd been brought up. He'd had a reputation for being a bit of a boozer. At church receptions he was known to knock back quite a few pints, and then start being extremely noisy. So I'd stereotyped all vicars as potential boozers. Just as I'd stereotyped all Swing into Shapers as boring. Wrong again.

When he'd gone Mike and I discussed what to do. Mike advised me to not give the Jehovah's Witnesses any more listening time. They obviously had their beliefs but they did not fit in with our own beliefs.

It was about a week later when the doorbell was rung again by the same two J.W.'s. As a Christian believer myself, it seemed strange to be in disagreement with two such sincere believers. I thanked them for coming again. I thanked them for having spent so much time talking to me about the Bible. Up to our last talk I'd found it most enjoyable. But I told them that I couldn't accept their interpretation of life after death. It was totally contrary to my own. I told them that I'd had the vicar round to discuss his interpretation and I preferred his to theirs. I asked then not to come again because I didn't want to waste their time. I felt bad about doing this. I felt so impolite, so rude - asking someone not to visit me. I couldn't remember asking anyone to do anything like this ever before. But I knew I had to. They were really nice to me and said goodbye with such sincere smiles. I felt awful as I closed the door, but relieved that now I could just continue to picture my Lydia in Heaven, with Jesus. It was what I needed to see.

You see, to have a picture of her in my mind's eye was most important to me. In all her short life I always knew exactly where she was. She was in S.C.B.U., then the Chapel of Rest, then the Funeral Directors, then the Crematorium. After that, Heaven. I needed this picture, it was vital to me. I had to be able to see her somewhere. Those J.W.'s just didn't know what they'd done to me to shatter my picture. But it was all over now, thank God.

Towards the end of February 1987 I started to go and have a cup of coffee with either Gill or Sylvia pretty regularly. They were both excellent listeners and I needed to talk, oh so very much. Talking really did seem to release some of the tension inside me. Gill and Sylvia must have listened to the same sob story time and time again and they were so good to me. They never made the sort of insensitive comments which some people had done - not that these people had meant to do so, I hasten to add. Sylvia and Gill would just listen to me.

Sylvia was the first one to start my thoughts moving away from "poor old me" to something completely different. One day, March-time, I'd just finished moaning about my lot and was saying cheerio to her. When Sylvia had walked out of the door, she turned round, looked me straight in the eye and said "You need Jesus". Then she turned and went. I was stunned. What on earth did she mean? I need Jesus. Why on earth should I need Jesus? He was in Heaven with my Mum and perhaps my Dad and Lydia. I was baffled. Me - need Jesus? What could she possibly mean? I carried on as normal, but every now and again I'd get this picture of Sylvia saying "You need Jesus" coming back into my mind. It intrigued me. Why on earth do I need Jesus? He looks after dead people, doesn't He? Not people who are still alive.

The next time she came, her parting words were the same - "You need Jesus". When she said it, it was as if someone was tugging at my heart strings. Why should my heart feel all funny at the mention of the name of Jesus? It seemed silly. It didn't make sense.

CHAPTER SEVEN

Jesus Loves You, Dot

At this time I was seeing Gill one week, Sylvia the next. I really enjoyed their company. They were "nice" people to be with. I could talk to them. About anything and everything.

One day, as Sylvia left, she handed me a little booklet called "What's the point?" which was all about finding the answers to life's questions from a Christian viewpoint. It was quite an informative book and, as I skimmed through the contents, I hungrily searched for the section entitled "Why is there so much suffering?" It did answer some of my questions, but not all of them. I could accept that no one is born perfect, but I found it difficult to accept that I'd had to have the baby with Down's Syndrome. I felt that I'd been picked on, possibly because I'd done some wrong things in previous years. I found it difficult to accept that a loving God didn't want any suffering, because I was suffering so much, and so had Lydia.

However, I must not neglect to mention two things that pulled at my heart strings yet again. First, just inside the front cover Sylvia had written "To Dot, love from Sylvia," and had drawn a very simple face with a big smile on it and underneath it were the words "Smile, Jesus loves you!" When I saw that, tears sprang to my eyes. Jesus loves me! You must be joking! He can't. He gave me Lydia and I didn't want her, well not the way she was. And He'd got my Mum when I wanted her. How could Jesus love me? Anyway, what's all this Jesus loves me stuff. He's in Heaven. That's where dead people are. He went up to Heaven at Easter time in 33 A.D. didn't he? What was Sylvia going on about? But whenever I thought of that name - Jesus - I felt all emotional and really had to hold back the tears. I didn't know why. It wasn't fair. He had the people *I* wanted. What was it all about?

Second, there was a note inside which read;

Dear Dot,

Please accept this little book with love. I could tell you such a lot about what Jesus means to me and my family, but I don't want to seem pushing! So, I'll just say that Jesus loves you Dot and your lovely family too! Where to start - well I suggest to start with prayer. Just ask the Lord where to start and He'll tell you, I know.

love Sylvia.

When I came to the sentence which read "Jesus loves you, Dot," I cried somewhere deep inside me again. Jesus. He loves me? Then why was I hurting so much? He had the ones I loved and wanted to carry on loving, here on earth. If He really loved me, why had He caused me so much pain by taking my Mum, my Dad and Lydia away from me? And just what was going on inside me? I felt so ridiculously vulnerable whenever the name of Jesus was being mentioned. I was thoroughly confused and frustrated.

In March, I discovered that I was pregnant again. I was so thrilled and yet so frightened. I did so want a little girl. Mike was sort of pleased about it, but wary. Who wouldn't be, with a 1 in 100 chance of having a mentally handicapped child growing inside his wife? He was very supportive to me, as he always has been and I know always will be. I've got a super husband.

What about Sam in all this? He was fast approaching four and he really was receiving very changeable care from his mother. Sometimes I was spoiling him rotten, sometimes I was neglecting him. Poor child. When I think now of all that he'd gone through in his short life. He'd started from being an eight week premature weakling, having been put on a drip to delay his arrival into this world, then put on another drip to be brought into it. He'd been given to a woman who wasn't prepared for him and who was consequently in shock for the first few weeks of his life. He then came home to be treated as if he was in a bubble, because of his prematurity and the fact that he was our firstborn. Then he gets his nose pushed out by the arrival and departure of Lydia. And now I was slowly ruining the child, letting him get away with things a four year old shouldn't be allowed to. In my depression, I was so inconsistent in my dealings with him. What is it we're supposed to be? Consistent, persistent and insistent. How I must have confused and upset him. What a mess I was making of being a mother.

And now I was pregnant again. I received quite amusing reactions from friends and family when I told them. It was a look of 50% pleasure and 50% horror from quite a few. They didn't know what to say - again. It wasn't the usual "Oh marvellous news, how lovely" situation at all. It was rather a question of "They've got Sam, had problems with Lydia. Shouldn't they, perhaps, be calling it a day and just sticking with one?" I knew all that, but I wanted a daughter. It had become an obsession.

Whilst all this was happening, Mike had been job hunting and had found a new job at Loughborough, a small town nearby, with a company making cranes. His job title was Design Manager. He started his new job on 27th April.

Whilst all this was going on, we were going through a legal problem with our neighbours. When we'd moved, we'd decided that we'd build a garage onto the side of our house. Now, in our deeds it said that we had to give our neighbours "reasonable" access to maintain their property. Our problem was the definition of "reasonable". I don't want to go into all the details. It's not necessary. Suffice it to say that we were at total loggerheads with our neighbours and it had all started to turn quite nasty. Now I know that, statistically, one in eight households do not, as the result of some problem, have a friendly relationship with their neighbour. O.K., I can accept statistics. But when you're a statistic, it's not very nice, especially when you've got other problems. I got very uptight about it all. Even to mention the neighbours' names made my blood boil. I had a very short fuse at that time. I'd moved to keep my mind preoccupied with other things besides Lydia. Now that I'd moved, I just wanted to grieve for her. I'd discovered that I was also grieving for my Mum and Dad and was up to my elbows in tissues. And now I had this, it was too much.

I know that Jean, the neighbour, was upset by it all as well. She was seeing the doctor because it had affected her nerves and was causing bad pains in her back. Well, as far as I was concerned, I felt she'd brought it on herself through being unreasonable. So she wasn't going to get any sympathy from me. I was suffering, so why shouldn't she. Oh, you bitch, Dorothy. And to think - I called myself a Christian!

Whilst all *this* was going on, I had yet something else to contend with. I was pregnant. My G.P., Dr. Spencer, had asked me to go to see a Mr. Liu at the City Hospital. He had discovered a way of testing babies for abnormalities at a very early age - when the foetus was only ten weeks.

We went to see him and he explained that, by taking cells from the sac surrounding the baby, he could, within days, get a result. Thus a mother could choose to have a termination, whilst not feeling too "pregnant". Also, the operation was so much simpler whilst the baby was still in its first trimester. If the baby was over twelve weeks, the birth would have to be induced and it would be far more traumatic for the mother and for everyone else.

Whilst I felt sure that there was nothing wrong with this baby, I felt that I should have this early test. It sounded a real answer to prayer. It wasn't. I was told that, after I'd had the test, I was to do absolutely nothing for a couple of days. Well, that was easier said than done. I had a son who was nearly four. Try telling him that his Mummy wasn't going to do anything for him for a few days. So I asked my twin sister, Margaret, if she would consider helping me. She said she would. I was really looking forward to her staying with me. We had real good heart to hearts whenever we got together, which wasn't very often, so the thought of her coming to stay for a few days was lovely.

So it was that on Thursday 30th April we both turned up at 9.30 a.m. at the City Hospital. Mr. Liu scanned me and told me that there was a problem. There were two sacs there. Twins! How wonderful! No, it wasn't quite like that. There were two sacs, but only one had a fertilised egg in it. He explained to me that this condition was not uncommon. In fact, statistically, it happened to 1 in 100 pregnancies. (I was getting rather fed up with being yet another statistic.) What normally happened is that the infertile sac would slowly disintegrate, leaving the fertile sac which had an egg inside it to thus produce just one baby. I thought perhaps that twins would have been a bit much to cope with. Then Mr. Liu came on to the problem. The unfertilised sac was blocking his vision of the fertile one. It was tricky enough doing the test with just one egg there. He didn't feel that he could manage it that day. He really needed to wait until the other sac had dispersed. I'd have to come back another day.

I couldn't believe it. What about Margaret having come here, away from her husband and the children? She'd gone to such a lot of effort to get down here to help me. I was bitterly disappointed. But there was nothing I could do. The timing was quite crucial as far as this test was concerned. Twelve weeks was the absolute limit. Mr. Liu looked at his diary for the following week. I asked if it could possibly not be the next week. My friend Sue Foster had won a free weekend in Paris for two and she had asked me to go with her. If I had to have complete rest after the test, then I would not be able to go. We decided that I should go to Paris and then come back on the Monday morning of my twelfth week. By then, hopefully, the empty sac would have disappeared.

Margaret and I went home. We tried to be cheerful, but I have to confess that, before she went home, I had a good sob on her shoulder. It was all pretty draining. I knew that there was a risk of miscarriage with this test, but decided that I just *had* to have it. I couldn't *not* have the test. Mike and I both needed peace of mind. We could not have gone through nine months of a pregnancy wondering if, at the end of it all, we'd have another mentally handicapped child. We'd have both cracked up. So Margaret went home. I went to Paris and had a lovely time with Sue. She's a very gentle, caring person and is good company.

Monday morning came. My wonderful friend, Annie, took me to the hospital. She'd volunteered to help me. She waited for me. I lay there. What was he going to say? Something good, I hoped. There was good news and bad news. The good news was that the sac had collapsed. The bad news was that it had collapsed around the sac with the baby in it. He couldn't get a clear view of the baby. He saw a line on the screen that should not have been there. Had something been left inside me during the trauma of Lydia's section, he wondered? It was not unknown. Emergency sections were not recommended, after all. Mr. Liu was very reluctant to do the test. In the end he said he couldn't make a decision. He left the decision making to me. What could I do? What a decision to make. If I said no, then what were the consequences? Well, I'd have to have an amniocentesis at sixteen weeks, and then wait four weeks to see if the cells had cultured. If they hadn't, then I'd possibly have to have another 'amnio', as two of my friends had. That would mean I could be 24 weeks pregnant before I knew whether or not I'd have to have an abortion! I didn't know if Mike and I could stand the tension for that long. One of the beauties of the test was that, once Mr. Liu had drawn off some cells, he would have taken it away, and returned within minutes with the knowledge that the cells were O.K. for analysis. And, of course, we'd have known the full result within a week.

If I said yes, there was, in Mr. Liu's opinion, a much higher risk of miscarriage. I can't remember the percentage, but it was pretty high. He told me to go and have a cup of coffee, then come back in half an hour and tell him.

I sat there with my cup of coffee like a zombie. I didn't know what to do. I couldn't 'phone Mike. He was out for the day. It was to be my decision and mine alone. What was I going to do? It all went round and round in my head until I felt dizzy. In the end I decided that I couldn't go through with it. I couldn't openly put my baby through a test which had such a high risk factor and which might result in the possibility of a miscarriage, when, in my heart, I was willing that this child would be perfectly all right. I'd have to have an amnio, that was the answer.

I gave Mr. Liu my decision. He accepted it. We decided that we'd try one last time on Thursday. So I went home feeling miserable and very sorry for myself.

On Thursday Mike came with me. It was good to have him there. My prop. And boy, did I need some propping! Onto the couch again. Things were still not good. The line had disappeared. Perhaps it had been something wrong with the monitor. Who knows? But the empty sac was still wrapped around the fertile one. It all looked pretty hopeless. I felt better, though, having Mike with me. We all decided that it was "no" again. It would have to be an amnio. We went home fed up. Why did life have to be so complicated?

I must not fail to mention that I was getting some help with coping with "my lot" from outside my circle of family and friends. I can't remember how, but I'd been told about a support group for the likes of me. It was called the Stillborn and Neonatal Death Society - SANDS for short. I still had this need in me to unburden myself onto as many people as possible, because I couldn't cope with it on my own. So I'd 'phoned SANDS. I was given the 'phone number of a member, Kate, who'd had a daughter with a chromosome disorder who'd died very young. She might give me some help.

I arranged to go to her house in Sherwood, which is a district of north Nottingham. She was to become a good friend. I went there on the 22nd April. This was a week before I'd had my first appointment with Mr.

73

Liu. We exchanged stories. Her story was not dissimilar to mine. Her daughter had not had Down's, but a much rarer chromosome disorder. The chances of having her daughter were extremely slim. Yet it had happened. It was good to share mutual feelings. She had not rejected her daughter as I had, but had accepted her child as "her lot", and had taken her home after only a few days. I really admired her for that. I cried a lot that evening. On leaving, I arranged to attend their next monthly meeting. Something happened, though, to stop me. I'll explain later. When I left Kate's house I felt a bit better at having shared my load again and at having opened a door to meet more people with similar experiences, who could give me comfort. I felt that I must have been driving my mates spare always wanting to talk about poor old Dot. Quite often I'd gone out determined not to talk about myself. But it didn't turn out that way. Something or someone would trigger me off.

The evening after my disappointing time with Mr Liu I started a nine week Confirmation Course. I was quite happy attending it. It seemed a natural thing to do. When I was a baby, I'd been dutifully Christened. I hadn't know that, when one is older, one is supposed to be Confirmed. It had been lacking in my education, somehow. I was quite prepared to be confirmed, though, if that's what Christians are supposed to do.

Graham, the vicar, led the course, which consisted of one hour of his teaching, followed by another hour when you could stay behind and ask questions. He gave everyone a sheet of notes to take home afterwards for reference. I found it all quite fascinating. There were about ten of us there, plus Graham. A mixed bunch, children and adults. And what Graham began to teach me was a real eye-opener. I thought that I'd had a pretty good Christian education, which had included going to Sunday School at the local Pentecostal Church every week without fail until the age of thirteen. But there were some quite startling revelations waiting for me each Thursday evening. I will describe each session, individually. Perhaps, as you read on, you will discover a revelation for yourself!

Session 1 was an introduction to what confirmation is all about. It was all new to me. I had never been taught anything about it. I discovered that it's a religious ceremony in which three main events would take place. One - I would confirm the promises which my parents and godparents had made on my behalf whilst I was a baby. (I had to smile - I don't know even now who my godparents are/were!). Two - the Bishop would confirm me

74

as a "full" member of the Church. Three - God would confirm (by filling me with His Holy Spirit) that I was now His daughter and heir, that my sins were forgiven and I would have eternal life. I didn't understand the last bit, but left it for Graham to explain later.

We looked at who God is and how we could know about Him. We looked at numerous verses in the Bible. For those people interested in the verses, I've made an appendix at the back of the book.

One verse in this first session was a sort of mini-revelation to me. It was Psalm 14:1, "The fool says in his heart "there is no God." Did God truly regard atheists as fools, I pondered? I have a friend, a truly lovely person who has been a great help to me, who is an atheist. Did God regard her as a fool? Well, there it was in black and white. Yes, He did. Should I tell her? Well, if she didn't believe in His existence, she'd probably just laugh at me anyway. I have, however, always acknowledged God. He'd always been there. The morning after my Mum's death, Dad told Margaret and me that she was with Jesus. After that, I'd accepted that there was a God. I couldn't believe in Jesus and not in God. The two had to co-exist. If there was no God, then where was my Mum?

In Session 2 we looked at why God created mankind in the first place, what the relationship is between God and mankind at present, and the reason for it. I found nothing here to make me re-evaluate my Christian stance. I warmed to the reasons why God created me, but found Matthew 5:16 a bit daunting when I looked at myself: "In the same way, let your light shine before men, that they may see your good deeds and praise your Father in Heaven." Now I'm the first to admit that I'm no angel, figuratively speaking, but the thought of men (and women) praising God in Heaven because of my deeds seemed extremely unlikely...!

We looked at the biblical reasons as to why I wasn't enjoying peace with God. It was summed up in one little word - sin. The Bible declared me a sinner. Romans 3:23; "for all have sinned and fall short of the glory of God." I had no reason to dispute this. Graham took us through the ten commandments (Exodus 20:1-17) and Jesus' teaching in the Sermon on the Mount, (Matthew 5-7) to help us to acknowledge ourselves as sinners. Yes, we all agreed with him, we're sinners all right. Graham had been very relieved that we had all so readily agreed that we were born sinners. He said that he'd really struggled with one group. But in this group there were quite a few parents of young children. We acknowledged that our children were quick to disobey us when given the chance. Born sinners! I went home that night feeling a 100% sinner. But not too upset, since I acknowledged that everybody else was born one as well!

We had been told that Session 3 would be the Good News after the Bad News of session two. However, I became very upset during session three. I know that I was pregnant, and that, hormone-wise I was up and down, but I ended up crying at one point. It just didn't seem fair.

You see, we began by looking at how, as a sinner, one could get right with God. The answer that the Bible gave was - nothing. To be right with God we had to do one thing and one thing alone - Acts 16:31; "Believe in the Lord Jesus and you will be saved."

So doing good without believing in Jesus just didn't get people to Heaven. I did believe in Jesus, so I felt O.K., but my thoughts turned to someone who was very much in the news at that time. Bob Geldof had just spent a lot of his time, energy and effort in doing good. He'd been heavily involved in Band-Aid, which had raised millions of pounds to help the starving people of Africa. I personally felt that his good deeds would earn him a place in Heaven. I challenged Graham on this. "So you're saying, Graham, that, even though Bob Geldof has just about worn himself out raising money to save people from dying, unless he believes in Jesus he won't go to Heaven?" Graham made no comment. But of course, I was being unreasonable in challenging him. It was there in front of me in black and white, Isaiah 64:6, "All of us have become like one who is unclean, and all our righteous acts are like filthy rags." I was challenging the Bible. The Holy Bible. So I cried. I couldn't stop the tears. Perhaps Bob Geldof did believe in Jesus. Perhaps he knew Isaiah 64:6. Perhaps....

It was in this session also that I was taught that the word "believe", in this context had a much deeper meaning than I had previously thought. It means "be persuaded by, put your faith in, entrust yourself to". I had thought it meant the same as in "I don't believe in the existence of Father Christmas" or, "I do believe in the existence of Margaret Thatcher". This word was more far-reaching to me in its newly defined form. Did I believe in Jesus? Was I persuaded by Jesus? Did I put my faith in Jesus? Did I entrust myself to Jesus?

Well, I reckoned that I could be persuaded by Jesus, though I readily accepted that there were many gaps in my knowledge of what He was trying to persuade me to do! I was happy to put my faith in Jesus. I had no

76

reason not to do so. I was quite at peace with that one. But did I entrust myself to Jesus? That seemed a more demanding requirement. I wasn't sure about what it involved, exactly. I didn't question Graham about it. Better not ask, rather than appear ignorant, I thought, or risk getting upset again.

We finished the session looking at why we should trust in Jesus and who He is. I had no problems in accepting Him as the Son of God, sent by God to show us the way to Heaven. We looked at many verses.

I accepted without reservation all that the Bible said about the supremacy of Jesus. I learned that He was actually with God at the time of Creation. I found that quite fascinating. I had always believed that He'd appeared first on the scene when born of Mary in Bethlehem. But we read John 1:1-3 and 1:14; "In the beginning was the Word and the Word was with God and the Word was God. He was with God in the beginning. Through Him all things were made; without Him nothing was made that has been made.... The Word became flesh and made His dwelling among us. We have seen His glory, the glory of the One and Only, who came from the Father, full of grace and truth." These verses, along with others quoted at the back of this book gave a picture of Jesus being there with God at the Creation. I suddenly had a whole new concept of Jesus.

In Session 4 we looked at what Jesus' death had achieved for us. I perceived a more detailed picture of what entrusting myself to Jesus would entail. I also discovered that a phrase which had always made me cringe was, in fact, Biblical, spoken by Jesus, Himself.

They're each quite fascinating, but the verses which amazed me were John 3:3 and 3:7 and 1 Peter 1:23: "In reply Jesus declared I tell you the truth, no one can see the Kingdom of God unless he is born again....you should not be surprised at my saying "you must be born again", for you have been born again, not of perishable seed, but of imperishable, through the living and enduring word of God." Now that phrase "born again" to me had previously conjured up a group of religious fanatics belonging to a sect in America to be positively ignored and avoided at all costs. I thought it was just a trendy name used to label a cult of weirdoes. I had no idea that a born again Christian was someone who was being exactly how Christ wanted him/her to be. I was amazed that I'd never before managed to spot the term in the Bible.

77

I wasn't able to join the others for Session 5. I'll break off from the confirmation course to tell you why. It's a long story.

CHAPTER EIGHT

The Miscarriage

It was Monday 8th June. I was 16 weeks pregnant to the day. I was so relieved. Dr. Spencer had told me that the dangerous time for miscarriages was not in the first 12 weeks as I had been led to believe, but in the first 16 weeks. And today I was 16 weeks. I was so relieved I'd made it. Hurrah!

Sam was at nursery. I was in the garden hanging out washing. I felt a bit tight around my crutch, but wasn't too concerned. Suddenly, whoosh! my waters broke. I screamed, "Oh no, no, no, no! This can't be happening." I dashed into the house, cross legged, crying and shouting "No. No, not today, not today, please. Oh my baby, my baby." I dashed to the 'phone which was at the bottom of the stairs. I sat there, virtually upside-down. (I had a theory that, if the baby was still alive and I kept my legs pointing up the stairs, then it might stay inside me. Crazy!) And I cried. Tears of frustration, tears of anger, tears of grief. You name them, they were there. Perhaps the baby wasn't gone. Perhaps it was still all right. Please, God, please let it still be all right.

Then I stopped moaning. Of course it was dead. Don't be so stupid. Your waters have gone. Of course it's dead. Once the waters have gone, then that's it. Dead. I tried to pull myself together. Now what do I do? I 'phoned the surgery. I needed a doctor. I was having a miscarriage. Dr Spencer was out on a call. The receptionist would contact him immediately. She recognised my voice and sounded very upset for me.

Whilst I was waiting for Dr Spencer I thought, "Shall I 'phone Mike?" Is it the done thing to 'phone up one's husband when one is having a miscarriage? If one in three women miscarry, perhaps people in industry were fed up with wives 'phoning up their husbands to tell them to come home. I wondered what Mike could do with me once he arrived home. I

79

was trying to be calm and sensible, and trying hard not to over-react to what I knew was an everyday occurrence.

And then I blew. Of course I wanted Mike with me. I needed him. I wanted him to hold me and to reassure me. I grabbed the 'phone. The receptionist answered. Sorry, he's in a meeting. A wave of frustration went over me. Well, could I speak to his boss, please. It was quite urgent. Mike had only been at this company a few months. I'd never spoken to his boss before. I didn't know how he'd react. But I was now past caring. I wanted Mike to be with me. I took a deep breath, "I'm very sorry to trouble you but I'm Mike Houghton's wife and I'm four months pregnant and I'm having a miscarriage. I'd like him to come home, please.... because I need him." I waited. There was a ....pregnant pause.

"I'll go and tell him right away," he said.

"Thanks very much. 'Bye." I put down the 'phone, quite exhausted. What do I do about Sam? I 'phoned a friend, Maggie, who had a child at Sam's nursery. She said she'd take Sam to her house and look after him until Mike came to fetch him. What about Mike? I 'phoned his parents. His Dad answered. I explained to him what was happening, and asked him to contact Mike later on, since Mike might need some help with baby-sitting. He was full of sympathy for me and said he'd do whatever he could. Good old Lofty. He is *so* nice. That's an understatement.

Dr. Spencer arrived. He 'phoned for an ambulance. He was most sympathetic. He'd seen me through all the Lydia trauma. He knew how disappointed I was. He said that the baby might still be alive but I knew it wasn't. It was dead. It had to be. My waters had completely gone. No baby. I told him so.

Mike arrived. It was wonderful to see him. I needed him. It was such a relief to see him - that's another understatement. He held my hand tightly. Then the ambulance arrived. I still clung on to his hand. There's not much else you can do when you're being carried out in a chair to an ambulance.

Our next door neighbour, Jean, appeared. She said that if there was anything she could do, Mike was to let her know. She hoped that our dispute had nothing to do with the miscarriage. I hadn't even thought about our dispute. That was the last thing on my mind. Of course our dispute had nothing to do with the miscarriage.

I was in the ambulance, Mike was following in his car. I thought, "This is the third time he's seen me going from the house in an ambulance with its lights flashing, and the second time he's been following one." Poor old Mike. What am I putting him through? Perhaps I shouldn't have dragged him away from work.

The ambulance man was trying to be as cheerful as possible. "We'll get you there as soon as we can. You'll be all right, don't worry. They'll do what they can for you. I'm sure your baby'll be all right."

"No, it's not," I said, quite firmly, but friendly, "You see, my waters have gone, completely. The baby's dead, it's gone. I'm all right, though, I've accepted it." He tried to look cheerful, but you can't when someone's just said what I'd said. So I chatted to him about Sam and what a super boy he was. That I was very lucky to have him. That I'd be all right once I'd got over it all. Isn't it amazing how one can put on a brave face at a time like that? But one does.... n'est-ce pas?

We arrived. The men wheeled me to reception with the papers given to them by Dr. Spencer. "Right," said the woman behind the desk, "if you'd like to take her down to Delivery, please." I started. Delivery? What's she talking about. The men looked uneasy.

"Delivery?" I asked. "Why Delivery? I'm here to have a miscarriage, not give birth."

"Well, it says on the papers to take you to Delivery, so that's where you're expected." The men looked even more uncomfortable. "Will you take her there, please?" she asked.

So they dutifully and reluctantly wheeled me along those familiar corridors, which I remembered most vividly, to the Delivery Suites. This seemed pretty cruel to me. I felt I had enough inside as it was, without all this as well. We arrived at Delivery. And waited. A midwife appeared and took my papers.

"I'm in the wrong place," I said. "I've come to have a miscarriage, not give birth. The baby inside me has just died." I wasn't hysterical, but I was getting very frustrated. Those poor ambulance men looked more and more uncomfortable. The midwife went away and a short time later another midwife approached me. "I'm so very sorry, my dear, they shouldn't have brought you here. They should have taken you up into the main wards." She turned to the ambulance men. "Could you take her up to Ward D39, please?" Once again she apologised to me.

"It's all right," I said, "it wasn't your fault." The ambulance men, with great relief, wheeled me away. I arrived on the ward with mixed feelings. "I've been here before," I thought. I was placed in a bed right in front of the staff's desk. There I could see a doctor just sitting there. Perhaps he was the one who was going to examine me. I waited. Mike arrived. I told him about going down to the Delivery Suite. He was not unduly surprised! We waited for someone to come and look at me. After what seemed a long time, a nurse came and tagged me, i.e., put a name label around my wrist. She said a doctor would come soon to see me. She was wrong. The doctor was still sitting at his desk. I kept glaring at him hoping that it would spur him into action. He didn't budge, but just sat there, having the occasional chat to a nurse. Even Mike, the epitome of patience, was getting a bit fed up of waiting. I wanted a doctor to examine me. I wanted him to say that I could go and sit on the loo and get rid of this dead baby that was inside me. And the sooner he did it, the better I'd be. I wanted to get rid of the baby and then go home. I'd had enough of this place already.

It was over an hour before a doctor saw me. He told me that I'd have to have a scan before I was allowed to do anything else. He didn't even examine me. There was a possibility that the baby could still be alive. So I was to do absolutely nothing that could endanger the baby's life. So when would I go down to be scanned? It would probably be in a couple of hours. They were busy. So I waited. I told Mike to go home. There was no point in waiting with me. I'd prefer it if he'd go home and look after Sam, then come back in the evening. So off he went.

I lay there, thoroughly cheesed off with the whole business. I cried a bit. It was mainly tears of frustration, I think. I'd shed my tears of grief back home. Why did I have to lose the baby today? Today of all days, just when I'd reached the sixteenth week. It just wasn't fair.

A very long time later, a nurse came to see me. "I'm very sorry to have to tell you this, but Scan can't fit you in tonight, they're too busy. We'll put you down for first thing tomorrow morning."

I could *not* believe it, I really couldn't. "You mean I've just got to lie here all night with my dead baby inside me. Can't I just go and get rid of it?" I was simply amazed at the thought of having to wait so long.

"I'm sorry, there's nothing I can do." And she left me. Well, what could I do? Nothing, absolutely nothing. I felt absolutely helpless.

Mike came that evening. His Mum was baby-sitting. He couldn't believe I hadn't been scanned. And yet he could.

Morning came. I waited. A nurse eventually came to see me. "They're too busy to fit you in this morning, you'll be going down this afternoon." I could feel my blood starting to boil. This could *not* be happening. It just couldn't. It was a nightmare. I 'phoned Mike. He said he'd come in the afternoon. It was a good job he did. I eventually got down to Scan at about 4 p.m. Mike wheeled me down there in a wheelchair. I don't know if any of you know the Q.M.C., but there is only one area for scanning, and that's the antenatal. (Things may have changed since 1987 though, I hope so.) I had to join the queue of women waiting to be scanned. Pregnant women. Lots of them. There was a sea of happy, smiling, expectant (forgive the pun) faces. And there was me. In my wheelchair. And Mike. He looked at me and pushed me to the front of the queue. "My wife's had a miscarriage and has been told to come for a Scan. She's not sitting here with all these pregnant women. I want her scanned now, please," he said in his "I'm not going to take no for an answer" manner.

The nurse looked rather taken aback. She hesitated. She didn't look very happy at all about it. "All right," she grumbled.

Mike wheeled me in. I knew this room, it was where I'd been scanned when I was having Lydia. Lydia! I felt as if someone was stabbing a knife into my heart. That pain again. Would it start all over again? Oh no, please God, no. I lay down on the couch. The staff looked really uninterested in me. They scanned me. "Yes," said one miserable looking nurse, "They're dead." She showed no emotion. Nothing.

"They, what do you mean, they? There's only one."

"No, there are two," she said.

"No, there's only one. I've been seeing a specialist at the City," I explained, "and there are two sacs there, but only one has been fertilised." I could see that I might as well have been talking to a brick wall.

"No," she repeated, "there are two dead babies there."

"Two, but that's not possible."

Mike wheeled me back to the ward. But there couldn't be two. Mr. Liu had said that there was one and he was the expert. A nurse came to see us. She was lovely. She explained that a doctor would have to see me, and that I'd probably be given something to induce the babies, i.e., self-abort.

83

Since I was 16 weeks, I was in the second trimester, which meant that I would have to go through all the natural process of childbirth to get rid of them. I was quite shocked at this. I hadn't expected anything like this. So I had to give birth? I shuddered at the thought of it. How can one give birth to something that was dead? How was I going to manage it?

The doctor came. He, too, was lovely. I explained to him that the nurse on Scan had said that there were two babies, but that Mr. Liu, the expert, had said that there was only one. He made no comment. A drip was set up for me. I'd been put into a side ward. I'd been told that things would probably start happening in the middle of the night. Well, they would do with me wouldn't they? It had been a middle of the night job with Sam and Lydia, so why not with this one? Mike left me. Poor old Mike. I felt so sorry for him. All he wanted was for me to be happy, yet every time I got pregnant it ended with him rushing to and fro from hospital with a load of hassle.

I felt it was easier for me, being in hospital, knowing what was happening. It was more difficult for Mike. He couldn't be with me. He had to go home and all he could do was worry about what was happening to me. At least I *knew*.

It was the middle of the night. I needed to go to the loo. So I sat on it with one of their paper commodes inside the loo bowl. They look rather like cowboy hats. I've always felt a desire to put one on my head, rather than sit on it! The baby started to come out. Quite naturally. It was fed up being inside me. It had been forced to stay inside me much longer than nature had intended it to. I stayed there quite a while and then buzzed for a nurse. She helped me back into bed and went to fetch a doctor. He wasn't long in coming and he was lovely.

I explained to him what had happened and that I was supposed to have two babies inside of me, but actually there was only one. I was getting fed up repeating this story, but felt I needed to tell them all, just to make sure that they knew what was happening.

He examined me, and my paper bowl. It was a good job I was used to all this by now. It could have been quite sickening if I hadn't already gone through what I had experienced with Sam and Lydia.

"What's in the bowl?" I asked.

"Do you really want to know?" he asked, looking up from it.

"Yes please, it's my baby, you know."

84

"Well, what we've got here are..... the legs." I felt sick. "You see," he explained, "When a baby of 16 weeks dies inside you, it starts to disintegrate. And that's what's happening. The rest of the baby will come soon."

He left me. He took the bowl away and left me with another. "Well, you did ask him, didn't you?" I thought. "Thought you could take it, didn't you? Perhaps you're not as tough as you make yourself out to be after all."

I lay there and waited. It wasn't long before the rest of the baby came. And then I started haemorrhaging. Quite badly. The nurse told me that she didn't like the look of it at all. She had been hoping that the second baby would come soon after the first. I told her that there wasn't another baby. It was just an empty sac. She wasn't listening to me. Why wouldn't anybody listen to me? She decided to call for a doctor. I was in a bad way. Clot after clot was coming out of me. Another doctor arrived. He said I needed to go to theatre. There they'd do a vacuum on me. By that he meant the same as an operation to abort a baby. Or, they might get away with a D & C, which would be gentler on me. But if there was a baby there, then it would have to be a vacuum.

"I'll only need a D & C then," I told him, "because there isn't another baby there. It's just an empty sac. Mr. Liu from the City hospital told me."

He wasn't listening to me either. Off I went to theatre. Again. Yet another nightmare. But not really, because I'd given up even trying to think about anything. I'd had enough. They could do with me what they wanted. They could donate my body to scientific research if they wanted to. I just wanted to go home and be with Mike and Sam. And I wanted my Mum. But I couldn't have her.

I woke up. I was still alive.

Back on the ward a doctor came. A different one. He looked at my notes. He didn't seem as friendly as the other doctor. "Well, Dorothy, they decided against the D & C for you and performed a vacuum. But they need not have bothered. There wasn't another baby."

"Oh, forget it," I thought.

"Now, the baby you gave birth to...." he paused. "It would appear that it had no legs." I turned away.

No comment.

I went home. Life carried on. It does somehow, doesn't it? Friends and relatives were kind, naturally. They were sympathetic. Some brought

85

me flowers. Some brought me chocolates. I moaned to some of them, put on a brave face with others, cried with some, couldn't be bothered to do anything with others. It all depended on what mood I was in. I was pretty moody at that time. Wouldn't you be? Sam started to get inconsistent parenting from me yet again. Just what was I doing to the poor child? Mike never knew what he was coming home to. Neither did I. I was a mess.

I remember being really bitchy to Julie, a Christian who had prayed for God's blessing and protection on my baby. "Those prayers you prayed were pretty useless, weren't they?" I almost sneered at her. She made no comment. A rare occurrence for her.

Five days after the operation, my milk came. I wasn't prepared for this. No one had told me to expect it. I told my health visitor. She told me that it did sometimes happen but that they didn't like to mention it beforehand, lest women get too upset thinking about it.

It seemed so cruel to me, to have this milk for my baby who'd died. Cruel also because I'd had to work at getting my milk to come for both Sam and Lydia. For this dead child, I'd made no effort. And look what nature had done. I missed him/her so much. So very much. I missed feeling pregnant. I liked feeling pregnant. I'd felt so complete, so fulfilled. Life seemed to be so cruel to me. Why was I suffering so much? All I wanted was a daughter. Was that too much to ask for?

Something quite startling was revealed to me after my miscarriage. There was no difference in my emotions between the loss of Lydia and the loss of this 16 week old foetus. None whatsoever. The post-natal effects on my body were the same - my breasts had been ready to feed a child both times. The only difference was that I had been able to hold Lydia, to grow used to her, and to begin a relationship with her. With the miscarriage there was exactly the same feeling of loss - the total abhorration of a loss of life. All my dreams had been shattered. It was irrelevant that Lydia had been there for all to see, and that this miscarried foetus was not a tangible creation. The expectations had been the same. The pain was the same. In one sense it was worse this time. People didn't seem so sympathetic with a miscarriage as they had been with a living baby. And my arms felt *so* empty. I had nothing to hold. At least I had been able to hold Lydia. I was surprised that the two deaths had identical effects on me. I'd spoken to Idris about how sad I felt that this child would not be recognised in the way that Lydia had been. We discussed the possibility of holding a service for the death of the baby. It seemed morally right to do so. Yet I didn't. I thought that people might think I was going over the top. People....me...

CHAPTER NINE

Love Hurts

I rejoined the confirmation class for Session 6. Graham gave me the handout for Session 5. I read it. I understood and agreed with the first part, but couldn't understand the second. The former talked of repenting. I'd always thought that to repent meant simply to say "Sorry." I hadn't realised it meant also deciding to turn from my old ways to God's ways - yet another gap in my education! There were lots of Bible verses to refer to, but I don't believe I looked at them. I was becoming very depressed after the miscarriage and had little motivation to do anything other than that which was absolutely necessary.

The latter part of the hand-out referred to the receipt of, or being baptised with the Holy Spirit. Now, I have to confess that I knew very little about the Holy Spirit. I suppose that, when I considered Christianity, I thought about God the Father and Jesus, the Son, fullstop. That the Holy Spirit is part of God, a gift from God to me, was a new and difficult concept to grasp. I was reminded of a hymn we often sang in school assemblies, in which the last line of one verse was "God in three persons, blessed Trinity". "Holy, holy, holy" was the hymn. So I remembered singing about the Trinity, but I'd never thought about what it actually meant. So, God was God the Father, Jesus the Son and the Holy Spirit. Fair enough.

The handout quoted many verses about being baptised in the Holy Spirit and said that being filled with the Holy Spirit was an event I would know about when it happened, either before, during or after my confirmation. Well I couldn't say I was filled with the Holy Spirit just then, because I felt so utterly miserable. I didn't know what to expect, nor was I motivated enough to go out looking for this experience. So I dismissed it. That's always the best approach to something baffling, isn't it? Ignore it and it will go away.

That evening, Session 6, the theme was the Christian hope. It seemed ironic to be looking at the resurrection of the body, of the dead, when my baby had only died ten days previously. Would I really see him or her again, perfect?

My baby had literally broken up. But I was comforted here tonight to read that God would recreate my baby. I looked forward to that day. I looked forward also to seeing Lydia again, perfect.

I had previously envisaged that, almost immediately after Jesus was raised from the dead, He went up to Heaven to be with God, and did not perform any more miracles. I'd thought that He only performed miracles before His resurrection. But after reading Acts 1:3 and other verses, I realised that after the Resurrection He was around for forty days, eating, drinking, talking, walking through doors, disappearing and performing miracles. When we talked about Jesus going up into Heaven, it was amazing to try and conjure up a picture of Him going up into the sky before the very eyes of His disciples. Incredible! Yet there I was reading it: Acts 1:9. That it happened I did not doubt. I'd just not thought about it deeply before.

We finished the session with something that was completely new to me. I had never been taught that, at some time in the future, Jesus would come back to earth with fire, that He would judge everyone, and that God would create a new earth that would be perfect - full of Christians.

I didn't know any of this. I'd somehow imagined life on the planet Earth going on ad infinitum. That people, once they were dead, were judged and then went to Heaven or Hell. I'd somehow got a picture of three places existing at one time - Heaven, Earth and Hell, in descending order.... So there actually is a date set, sometime in the future when it's all going to end. And then there'll just be two places - Earth, which will be inhabited by Christians, and Hell. Gosh. I felt frightened. Perhaps it would be very soon. I wasn't looking forward to it. We looked at the Bible verses. I didn't like what I was reading at all. I thought about my atheist friend, my family. Did they know? I'd thought that all that talk about "Armageddon" by Jehovah's Witnesses and those "The end of the world is nigh" placards were all a load of rubbish, a way of frightening people into

89

changing their ways. I'd never taken them seriously, just laughed at them. But right now I wasn't. I'm glad I'm a Christian, I thought.

Session 7 seemed pretty mild, compared to the previous one. This session was entitled "The Church" and it looked at the importance and necessity of joining and attending a Church.

I cringed a bit at Hebrews 10:25 "Let us not give up meeting together, as some are in the habit of doing, but let us encourage one another - and all the more, as you see the Day approaching." I remembered the previous session. I didn't like thinking about "The Day".

We looked at the reasons why we should go to Church. They were all extremely positive. I was already enjoying going to Church each Sunday evening, and always felt better in some way when I came home. The session was essentially on "selling" attendance at Church, through looking at the Scriptures. It was good. I bought it.

I certainly was getting comfort through going to Church. Don't ask me to explain how - I just was. I enjoyed the singing. I liked the idea of being close to God, I felt close to Him there, on my knees in prayer. Yet why should this comfort me when He'd got my children and my Mum and Dad? It was strange. He scared me, He had such power. Was I so bad that I'd had to lose both parents and children? "Oh God, don't let me have to lose any more people I love. Please." I cried such a lot in Church. It was grief and self pity. And yet, when I went home, I always felt better for it, with a little more strength and energy to get through the next week. I did need to go to Church.

Session 8 looked at the subject of taking Communion - the eating of bread and drinking of wine. I learned that it would be "my duty" to receive Holy Communion regularly, "especially at Christmas, Easter and Whitsun" - Canon B 15 1 (whatever that was!). So that would get me to Church at least three times a year!

The last two Bible references struck a chord of fear in me. They spoke of the danger of my receiving Communion if not right with God or my fellow believers. Dare I take it? There were people I didn't feel right with. And, was I right with God? I wasn't sure. Perhaps I shouldn't take Communion. But I did want to be right with God and with others. Perhaps that was good enough. Perhaps not. Most probably not.

Session 9 was in the form of a questionnaire. We were posed detailed questions challenging us on issues relating to what we would be declaring on the evening of our Confirmation - if we were to go through with it. Did I believe in God? Did I believe He created the world? Did I believe He created me? For a purpose? Did I agree I was to be accountable to Him one day for what I'd done? Was I willing to give up any known sins, to put things right where appropriate? To obey God from now on? Did I believe that Jesus alone could put me right with God? Did I accept that Jesus was Lord of everything? Would I commit myself into Christ's hands, acknowledge Him as my Lord and King, and submit to Him and His laws? Would I ask God to fill me with His Holy Spirit, to live in me? Would I ask Jesus to "baptise" me with the Holy Spirit? Would I try to find out what being a full member of the Church meant for me, as an individual? What part of the Church make-up did God want me to be?

We then had to sign on the dotted line, saying whether we felt ready to be confirmed or not, or whether we needed further discussion on certain aspects about Christianity.

I answered "yes" to all the questions and said, on paper, that I was ready to be confirmed. But I have to admit that, although without doubt I believed in everything we'd discussed, I was definitely wary about making Jesus my Lord. I felt apprehensive about submitting to Him. Wasn't this challenging my independence? I'd not had someone as my Lord before. My superior. Sure, I'd had my Dad, but that was different. I'd had no say in the matter. Here I was being asked to volunteer to have someone tell me what to do. It didn't seem a natural thing for me to volunteer for!

Yet, if I didn't become a confirmed member of the Church, then God wouldn't be happy with me. Being confirmed was the "right" thing to do. I had to do it. If I said no, I couldn't call myself a Christian, nor go to Heaven. So I duly handed in my form with a "yes" answer, whilst knowing in my heart that something wasn't quite right. I think that I was secretly hoping that the niggling feeling in me would quietly go away. It didn't.

Our last session, Session 10, raised some quite interesting facts for me. I suppose I'd just never thought about them before. I learned that, according to the Bible, I'm basically made up of three elements - body, soul and spirit. My soul, or mind, helps me to communicate with myself, and my spirit is for communicating with God. I never knew that. I'd always acknowledged my having a spirit of some sort, a very stubborn one at times, so my brothers used to tell me! I never knew that God had made the Holy Spirit available to me, to be an integral part of me, enabling me

91

to communicate with God. If I'm a sinner, then my spirit is dead, it can't communicate with God. It needs to be made alive - thus the need to be "born again." Then the Holy Spirit would guide my spirit into a growing relationship with God. It was quite mind-boggling stuff, but all quite acceptable to me in the light of our group discussion and the Bible verses which confirmed Graham's teaching.

Then we went on to see that the Holy Spirit, speaking directly to our spirit, would guide us through God's word, i.e., the Bible (pretty awesome thought, how could that happen I wondered), and through other people.

Prayer was an obvious means of communicating with God. I did pray. Not a lot. I had such a fear of His Power, of what I felt He'd already done to my family, or permitted to be done. Yet I didn't dare blame Him totally. I was too scared to blame Him for my lot. He was, after all, God.

We were encouraged to talk to God. It's funny, but I'd always found it easier to talk to my dead Mum when I'd needed help. Perhaps she was more approachable, in my mind's eye. But Graham's notes explained that it was going to be easier for me to talk to my Mum than to God. If I was a sinner, and not filled with the Holy Spirit, then I couldn't communicate with Him! If I was spiritually dead then I could only communicate with the dead, but if I was spiritually alive then I could communicate with the living God. It seemed so obvious once I'd been told the facts.

We finally looked at Spiritual Gifts. These are supposed to be for the benefit of the Church as a whole, so I was encouraged to join a Church House Group to discuss them there. These House Groups were groups of between six and ten Christians meeting weekly, to talk about Christianity. Graham didn't go into detail about Spiritual Gifts, other than read the Bible references. I don't think we could have taken much in that evening anyway. I personally was finding it very difficult to grasp the concept of" spiritual things," i.e., the Holy Spirit, my spirit, and spirits communicating with one another. So much so, that I could have chosen to give up on it all. It all seemed a bit beyond me, to say the very least. Yet another case of "I don't understand it so I'll dismiss it". Shame on me really. Me, a teacher, too. I always taught, "If you don't understand, then ask". I didn't understand this spiritual stuff and I wasn't asking.

Graham's teachings made me realise that I'd been very wrong to call myself a Christian. I just wasn't one, but I'd honestly and sincerely thought that I was. But at that time I had to confess that Christ wasn't my Lord. I could call myself a believer in His existence, but not a true follower of Christ.

I felt even more depressed. Life had been bad enough since the miscarriage, but to discover that I wasn't something that I'd always considered myself to be was yet another blow to knock me down, yet another nail to hammer into my already well hammered coffin.

It was Wednesday, 22nd July, the last day of school before the six weeks' holiday. Sylvia had asked me if I'd like to go to the Baptist church to attend a one-off Family Focus talk. The subject was the teaching in our schools. Would I be interested? I was quite happy to go.

That was until I walked through the door. There in the congregation was Julie, a Mum who had been pregnant when I was pregnant with Lydia, sitting there with her daughter. There also was another Mum, Margaret, with her son, about the same age as Lydia would have been. And Sharon, with her son. They all looked so happy. So frustratingly happy. I felt so angry. I wanted to scream and walk out. But I stayed. I could see that Julie knew I was upset. She kept away from me.

I listened to this woman giving the talk. It was all good stuff and I agreed in principle with everything she said was happening and not happening in our so-called Christian schools, locally and nationally. I learned that there were specially organised prayer groups, purely for our schools. I didn't, at that point, realise how powerfully these prayer groups could be used by God.

But, whilst I was listening to her, I had this awful ache inside me. I did so ache from the pain of seeing these Mums with their children. And they all looked *so* annoyingly happy. Why couldn't I be happy? It just wasn't fair.

I put on a brave face and walked home. The pain inside me was the worst it had ever been. I was two streets away from home and rounded the corner. There in front of me was yet another Mum who had been pregnant when I was with Lydia. My stomach turned over. She looked embarrassed, blushed, mumbled "Hello" and scuttled past me with her child. I knew that she didn't know what to say. She wasn't to be blamed. But it made me feel even more depressed. With the pain knotting my insides even more I turned into my street. And my stomach turned over once more. There was somebody else at the end of my street pushing, of all things, a pram. It wasn't fair. *I* should be pushing a pram. Why couldn't I? I didn't know this lady. She crossed the street. "That's it," I thought, "Go on, you treat me like a leper as well."

I walked into the house, sat down on the stairs and wailed. I had to talk to someone. I needed someone. But who? Who could help me? I couldn't think of anyone. My friends must surely have had enough of me. My relatives were just too distant, not only physically but also because we hadn't 'phoned each other much. So they didn't really know what I was going through. To have 'phoned them and off-loaded all my woes. It would have taken hours. I thought of Kate from SANDS. But no, she has her own life, her own tragedy. What right have I to 'phone her up and expect her to have time to listen to me? She could be enjoying a really good, happy moment. I couldn't destroy it for her. But right now I was being destroyed. It was awful.

So I sat on the stairs with the 'phone book on one side of me and the 'phone on the other, and I just cried and cried and cried. And it hurt, you know, like that hurt, that real aching, sobbing you used to get as a child when you'd hurt yourself and you couldn't breathe and were lost in uncontrollable gulps.

Just who could I talk to? I couldn't 'phone anyone. Not even Mike. He was at work. He mustn't be put on by me any more whilst he was there. He'd got enough to cope with. I felt so alone. I was desperate. "Please, God," I wailed, looking heavenwards, "Please, God, take away the pain."

The Saturday after I'd been to the Baptist church my sister's two children arrived to stay with us for a week. On the Sunday evening I asked Carrie if she'd like to come to the parish church with me. She came along. It was the Evensong service. I found it quite amusing to see and hear her reaction to our rather old-fashioned service. "There's a lot of getting up and down, Aunty Dorothy, isn't there?"

I smiled, wryly. "Carrie," I asked her, "Do you believe in God and Jesus?"

She blushed. "I don't really want to believe in them because, if I did, then I'd have to believe in the devil. And I don't want to."

Quite a good answer, for a 13 year old, I thought.

It was a Friday night. The people of the Baptist church were holding a ten week seminar on counselling, and I'd been going to most of the meetings. I'd found them all intriguing. Mike was quite happy to let me go. If it made me feel better, then he was all for it. This night was different from the rest. When I walked in I felt very moved by the atmosphere. I sat down on the back row. I had my bagful of tissues ready. There was something about that place that made me cry quite easily. It didn't bother me at all though. After all, Jesus cried. If it's all right for the Son of God to cry, then it's perfectly all right for me to do it, as far as I was concerned. I don't know why people have hang-ups about crying in public. Is it the great British stiff upper lip image that has to be adhered to that stops people having a good sob when they're upset? I've never had a problem with it.

The Minister, Peter Jackson, started us off in prayer. And I started to cry quietly. The tears just wouldn't stop. He kept talking about Jesus and how much Jesus loved us and how grateful we all were for His love. But, love, I was thinking, love hurts.

Peter stopped his opening prayer and then asked us all to be quiet and to wait to see if God had any word for us. There was a silence. I tried to be as quiet a crier as possible. And then a lady spoke. "I have a picture. A picture of a little girl, looking at a present in front of her. It's beautifully wrapped, and the little girl looks as if she daren't open it. She's just having a little peep at the gaps in the wrapping, but she daren't open it. She's afraid."

There was silence. Now, when she first said "little girl," the tears had literally shot out of my eyes, they'd leapt from me. I knew that it was me she was talking about. I was so 100% sure of it. I stood up defiantly. I knew that I had to respond. I dug my hands deep in to my coat pockets. "I am that little girl in the vision. And I tell you all right now," gritting my teeth, "that I am *not*," I emphasised this, "*not* going to open that box. Never. You lot say how wonderful it is to be a Christian and that life's great. Oh, I've had days when I've said prayers and had a good day, but then the next day has been awful. Full of pain and hurt. And you say you want me to give myself to Jesus, to love Him and make Him my Lord. Well, I tell you now, I'm not going to because when you give yourself 100% to people, they hurt you. And I don't want to be hurt any more, so I'm not going to."

I stood there, in my defiance, tears pouring down my cheeks. I didn't care, I was past caring about anything. I was worn out. I opened my eyes. There were people stood around me, praying. The lady who'd had the vision was one of them. My friend, Sue Playle, was another. She was holding onto my arm, crying as well. Others were praying, words I couldn't understand. But I wasn't bothered, I wasn't bothered about anything. I'd had enough.

When I walked home that night, I felt confused. Half of me was saying, "There, that told them." The other half was saying "Go on, open the box."

I was becoming more and more enveloped in deep depression. I couldn't be bothered to do much at all. I was going through the motions of being a wife and mother. I wasn't like some people with chronic depression who can't face doing anything at all. I was performing my wifely and motherly duties, but it was with the bare minimum of effort. I was so lethargic. Everything I did seemed to be a chore, to be performed with no enjoyment. To the outside world I probably looked O.K., but inside I was an absolute mess.

Now, if you've ever suffered from deep depression, you'll be able to identify with this. But if you haven't, you can't possibly imagine the despair. I remember once talking to a health visitor about someone who had post natal depression, and saying that I was sure I could understand how she felt. The health visitor turned and said to me "No, you can't because post natal depression is so debilitating that you can't really understand it unless you have experienced it." And now I had it, though I didn't know it at the time. It all made sense when one of the local G.P.s, Dr. MacLaren, identified it and put a label to my rather pathetic and forlorn condition.

I was so very low. Even though I had a wonderful husband and son, life to me was awful, because I'd lost my daughter and I'd lost another baby. And people weren't helping me in the way I felt I needed them to. They were surviving and I wasn't. They had parents to help them and I didn't. People seemed to have what they wanted and I didn't. In reality it wasn't like that at all, but to me, in my condition, that's how it felt. Even the television adverts kept thrusting in my face wonderfully happy families with the parents proudly holding onto their new-born child. I couldn't escape from babies anywhere.

What was I going to do? Life just didn't seem worth living. And then it came to me - why not commit suicide? Then I'd be out of all my pain and I'd be with Lydia, and with my Mum and perhaps with my Dad. Why not? Lydia wouldn't have anything wrong with her up in Heaven. And my

Mum wouldn't have cancer. I could remember the bit in the Bible which said that there'd be no tears or pain, only joy. It sounded a far nicer place to be than here.

And then I thought of Mike. What would he do without me? I shrugged my shoulders. Oh, he'd be all right. He could cope without me. He'd managed all right before he met me. He could cook and look after himself. He could get his Mum to do his washing for him again, like she used to. And he could marry again, if he wanted to. I'd found someone else to be happy with, he could do the same. He'd probably be happier with someone who wasn't as miserable as me. You might ask yourself how I could possibly consider killing myself when I had a husband who loved me dearly and who I professed to love? Well, when you're in a deep depression you don't think logically. I've since spoken to others who have suffered from a similar attack. They have admitted that they too have considered doing something totally illogical, positively suicidal, and extremely out of character. Yes, I'd kill myself.

And then I thought of Sam. I immediately stopped thinking about killing myself. I couldn't leave him without a Mum. I'd been left without a Mum and look how it had scarred me. No, I couldn't do the same to Sam. Also, I couldn't put the trauma of suicide into Sam's life. I couldn't let him grow up with any feelings of guilt about his mother committing suicide, wondering if he had had anything to do with my taking my life. I didn't want to hurt him. I loved him too much for that. I couldn't kill myself. I stopped thinking about suicide.

Well, what else could I do? If I carried on this downward spiral then I knew I was going to crack up. I'd then be no good as a wife or a mother. I might as well be dead as crack up. What could I do?

And there was this call to be a Christian. Everybody kept on telling me that Jesus wanted to help me in all of this. But Jesus was in Heaven. How could He help me to get out of this mess that I was in *on Earth*? It just didn't make sense. And another thing. They were all saying that, to become a Christian, I had to give myself totally and utterly to Jesus. I was to make Him my Lord and my Master, and I was to love Him with all my heart. Well I'm afraid that my heart was feeling a bit too raw to consider a masochistic donation of it to someone else, thank you very much.

I couldn't do it. It would hurt too much. But I knew that I had reached a critical point in my illness. I needed help. The tablets from the doctor weren't helping me. The brandy which I'd resorted to as a night-cap to try and help me sleep was adding to my depression rather than helping it. The SANDS group wasn't helping me in the way I needed help. The only escape I could see from this sorry mess was to become a Christian. But I *was* a Christian, wasn't I? Oh, it was all too confusing.

But here was this one olive branch being offered to me. I'd tried every other branch - friends, relatives, SANDS, and they couldn't give me what I needed to keep me sane. I had to go for it. So one day in September 1987 (I'm not sure which date exactly - I'm not like some Christians who can quote the date and exact time of their commitment to Jesus) I sat down on the floor in the lounge and took out another booklet that Sylvia had given me - "Journey into Life" by Norman Warren - and I said the prayer in it. I said sorry to Jesus for sinning in my thoughts, my words and my actions. And I told Him that I turned away from everything that I knew was wrong. And I asked Him to come into my life, as my Saviour. To cleanse me. To control me. To be my friend. And I promised to serve Him all the remaining days of my life in complete obedience. Then, suddenly feeling rather frightened, I added to it, "And please don't hurt me, Jesus."

And nothing happened. I still felt awful. Why? I wanted all my pain to go. My headache. My heartache. It was still there. Perhaps He wasn't listening. Perhaps He wasn't bothered about me. But I needed help. "Help me, Jesus, please."

A few days later, feeling no different, I dug out the booklet, got down on my knees and said it again, and said it louder, just so that He could hear me. He might have been busy elsewhere, perhaps. Oh, I just didn't know. It was all so silly anyway. As if He could hear me in my lounge!

That Sunday I went to St. Peter's Church. I sat about two thirds of the way down the aisle on the right. Gill came and joined me. Graham was praying. He was talking to Jesus. I was on my knees. I looked up at the huge wooden cross that is mounted on the screen and prayed inwardly, whilst crying inwardly as well. "Please, Jesus, please don't hurt me." The tears started to fall. I did hurt so. I did ache so.

And then, through my tears, I saw and felt a presence come down from the cross. Not a person. Dare I say - a ghost, a spirit. And He was next to me and He spoke to me. I couldn't see Him but I heard His words so very clearly. I remember them vividly to this day.

"You think that by loving Me you'll be hurt the same

way you were hurt by loving your Mum, your Dad

and Lydia.

But I'll never hurt you.

I love you.

I've loved you for a very long time.

I love you so much, I died for you."

CHAPTER TEN

Jesus

I didn't mention it to Mike. To be honest, I don't think that my conscious mind was aware of what had happened. But my spirit was. Jesus had healed my spirit. Indeed He had given life to my spirit, which previously had been dead. I knew inwardly that I was going to be all right. That I'd get better. That I wasn't alone any more. That I would no longer feel the pain that had become part of my very body. That aching, hurting feeling inside of me had gone, evaporated. I felt a total inner feeling of calm and peace. It was beautiful. I felt just so very, very, very much better. I could almost float, walk on air. That heavy weight on my shoulders, which had made me feel as if I carried all the troubles of the world on them, was completely and utterly gone. No longer did I feel that the whole world was against me, that nobody could help me, that I was going to sink lower and lower, and become more and more miserable to be with that I'd never be happy again.

And, in the days and weeks which followed I just talked to Jesus all the time. Because I knew He was there, that He loved me, that He wanted to help me, and that He wasn't going to hurt me. He'd told me so. And so I returned His love. I told Him all about my problems, even though I realised that He knew them already. I knew that He was listening. I knew that He was with me every single second of the day. So I talked to Him in the bathroom, I talked to Him in the kitchen. I talked to Him whilst I was walking back from taking Sam to school, I talked to Him whilst I was doing the cleaning and whilst I was driving. When I woke up first thing in the morning I'd say "Good morning, Jesus," and talk to Him whilst waiting for Mike to wake up.

It was a beautiful time in my life. I suppose that it was because things had been so awful until the Lord Jesus spoke to me that the change in me was so dramatic. From feeling so low, I was now on Cloud . walked around with my head held high, instead of being round shou. and downward looking. Life was so completely different.

Mike benefited immediately. He didn't get his ears so bashed now. I could off-load to someone else - Jesus. He didn't mind an ear-bashing. In fact, He wanted it. He wanted me to off-load all my moaning to Him. To get it completely out of my system. So that I could start all over again. And that's just what I did. And it was great.

Yes, Jesus was the answer to all my problems. Wonderful Jesus. He died for me. Me!! I was so important to Him. So special! I felt 100% loved. I felt cocooned in a blanket of His love. I felt all tingly, just like lovers feel when there are no barriers, when they've abandoned all their inhibitions and given themselves wholly to each other. Sheer ecstasy. It says in the Bible that Jesus is our lover, and boy, did I feel loved. I was so overwhelmed with His love, that I'd sometimes just sit and think about His love for me, and smile constantly, grinning like a Cheshire cat. I was so deliriously happy.

I cried, of course. That wouldn't have been me if I had not done so. But they were different tears. They weren't tears of hurt, frustration, anger, bitterness or pain. They were tears of joy, happiness, relief and love. I was *so* happy!

Now all of this did not in any way take away my affection for Mike. Let's face it, another man had come on the scene now. This could have caused a problem. But it didn't, not at all. On the contrary, I was now wanting to be more physical with Mike. Whilst I'd been so very depressed, my desire to make love had been pretty pathetic. But now everything was very different, because I was different.

Mike asked me what had happened. I couldn't explain it very well. All I could say was that I had now become a Christian, having realised that I hadn't truly been one before. That I felt so much better now. I didn't at that point tell him that Jesus had spoken to me, partly because my conscious mind wasn't fully aware of it yet. It was something that had happened deep within me, which hadn't yet reached the surface of my mind. It took a few weeks for this inner healing to become wholly apparent to me.

This might seem hard to understand. Perhaps I can compare it to a doctor giving you, say, antibiotics for a big infected sore on your hand.

You take the tablets, they go deep within your system and, gradually, over a period of days, reach the infected area and heal it. You can't actually feel these antibiotics working within your body, fighting against the infection. It's only when the tablets have actually treated the sore that you can appreciate what's been going on in your body. Just as those antibiotics take a while to surface in their healing, that's how I felt I was slowly being healed - with tender, loving care. It was all quite beautiful.

Now that I had someone to off-load my problems onto, life was wonderful. Mike and I were becoming closer again. Sam was happy at school. Life wasn't too bad at all! Oh, Jesus, what a life-saver You are!

But, I still wanted a daughter. What were we going to do? I'd been back to see Miss Jecquier, my gaenecologist, at the Queen's Medical Centre. She told me that there was no reason why I shouldn't have a perfectly normal pregnancy and delivery next time, and that I should be O.K. No, she wouldn't advise me *not* to get pregnant again - I'd be all right. I'd also been to see Mr. Liu at the City Hospital. His opinion was the opposite. He'd been quite concerned at what he'd seen of my insides when he'd scanned them. With my history he'd feel reluctant to advise another pregnancy. But he did assure me that, if I did become pregnant again, he'd do what he could for me. We also remembered that according to the Clinical Genetic Service, our chances of having another Down's Syndrome baby were one in 100, increasing more with my age.

So the dilemma was this. Should we try for another pregnancy, knowing that I'd want to have a test of some kind to see if I might have another Down's child? Knowing that Mr. Liu didn't like the look of my insides? Knowing also that Miss Jecquier would probably want to do a Shirodkar Suture yet again? Realising all the hassle of being hospitalised again in a hospital that wasn't exactly my favourite place? Accepting that Mr. Liu might not be able to perform his test? Knowing that I might have to have an amniocentesis, or two, to get a result? Did we really want all this? Well, no, we didn't. But I wanted a daughter. What were we going to do?

A friend told me that she and her husband were going to apply to adopt a child. She wanted a daughter and felt right considering adoption. I told Mike what they were doing and he became very interested in the idea.

"Perhaps we should think about adopting a daughter," he suggested quite eagerly. The thought of us having a daughter through adoption, without all the traumas of pregnancy, appealed to him and who can blame him? But I didn't fancy it at all. Someone else's child? I shuddered at the thought. No thank you. I didn't want that. I wanted my own child, from my own womb. I wanted that special bond that mothers have with their daughters. I couldn't possibly have that with someone else's child. No.

So it was stalemate. Mike didn't want me pregnant and I wanted to be pregnant. It could have developed into something that divorces are made of. We didn't argue about it. We had very rarely argued about anything. But there seemed to be no solution. But there was.

It was a Wednesday morning, I was attending a housegroup meeting at the Vicarage, near my house. I felt particularly worn out. What were we going to do? Sue Playle started the opening prayer and I suddenly felt moved to tears. I tried to hide the fact that I was crying. "Stop your crying, there are other people here besides you," I told myself. But I couldn't. I remember a fellow Christian, Jean Rogers, putting her arm around me, and then the tears flowed uncontrollably. I had a real good cry. I needed it.

"What is it?" asked Sue.

"Oh, I don't know what to do," I wailed. "I want a baby so much, so very much, but I just don't know what to do. I've got one specialist at the Queen's saying "get pregnant", and another at the City saying "don't". I've got Mike saying that he doesn't want me to get pregnant again and I can understand why. I don't blame him under the circumstances, but I want a baby. And I don't know what to do."

"What are your alternatives?" asked Julie Lazonby, who that day was leading the meeting.

"Well, we've got three really, I suppose: One, I get pregnant, which Mike doesn't want. Two, I don't get pregnant, and I don't think I could live with that. The thought of never being pregnant again, always wondering whether another pregnancy would have been fine or not. Or three, we try and adopt. Mike's quite keen on the idea. But I don't fancy it at all. I want my own baby, from my womb. I've been advised not to consider anything for at least three months when, in theory, my body should have got over the miscarriage. But it's on my mind all the time and I'm just worn out with it all."

Silence fell.

"Have you thought about asking God what to do?" asked Julie, gently.

I gave her one of my "What on earth are you talking about" looks. "Well, actually, Julie,.... no," I said, exasperated.

"Well why not ask Him?"

I looked at her condescendingly. "O.K., Julie, go ahead, ask Him. Ask Him what I'm going to do about it all. Yeah, go on."

So Julie prayed, "Heavenly Father, almighty God, we thank You for Dot. We thank You for Mike. We thank You for Sam. Please God, Dot doesn't know what to do about another child, but she'd like one. She has a decision to make from a list of three options. She needs help, Lord, Your help. Please tell her clearly, Lord, what to do. Make it crystal clear to her what *You* want her to do. Write it clearly across the skies so she can't miss Your answer and please, Lord, give Dot peace over all this situation and bless their household. Lord, we ask that you give Dot three months to get over her miscarriage, as the doctors have recommended, and then give her an answer. We ask this in Jesus' name. Amen."

"Amen," we all agreed. I'd accepted Julie's prayer rather tongue in cheek. Sure, God would tell me what to do! As if He could! That evening, when Mike came home from work, strangely I didn't feel the need to bring up the subject of having another baby. In fact we had a good laugh about it all.

"It's all right Mike. I'm not going to go on at you any more about becoming pregnant. This morning at the Vicarage we asked God to tell me what to do. In three months time He's going to give me the answer, when my body's back to normal.

"Oh good," he smiled. (It was a sort of a cross between a "thank goodness she's getting off my back," and a "she's finally cracked up" look.) "Well let's hope that God's of the same frame of mind as me."

We agreed that we would look at the possibility of adoption. I didn't want to. As far as I was concerned we were going to try for another one ourselves, because that was what God was going to tell me to do. But I agreed in principle to making initial enquiries.

"Now, how do you adopt?" I thought. "I know, I'll 'phone up the local Social Services at County Hall, West Bridgford. They'll know." West Bridgford's about three miles from Ruddington, and the administrative base for all the local services. So I did. "I'd like to talk to somebody about the possibility of adopting a child, please."

"Where do you live?"

"Ruddington."

"Ring this number." So I did.

Meanwhile, on the 6th October 1987 I was duly confirmed. The Church was packed. The now-deceased Richard, Bishop of Sherwood, was preaching. I found it all quite moving. I was quite surprised to see such a packed church. There were a lot of friends and relatives of the other candidates. "Gosh," I thought, "I didn't even think to ask any of my friends or family. I wonder if they would like to have come?"

It was Mike's first time in St Peter's Church since Sam's christening. The atmosphere was very much different from that which he'd experienced then. There was an air of expectancy tonight. He really enjoyed being there. Mike was very impressed with Richard. He didn't preach from the pulpit, but chose to preach from the aisle and shout his sermon to the congregation. He was a most sincere and exciting speaker. It was the first time that Mike had listened to such an inspirational preacher. He still talks of the influence that Richard had on him to this day. It was during the service that Mike thought it right to join the confirmation class the following year, to take a closer look at Christianity. He'd never looked into the Christian faith any more than the R.E. taught in school. He felt it needed investigating. If God wanted to have a personal relationship with him then he ought to at least make the effort to find out more.

When I went forward to receive the Bishop's anointing with water I'd been told by Graham that I could expect "something" to happen, that I could expect an anointing by The Holy Spirit. I felt nothing.

After the ceremony we all went for a cup of tea and a biscuit in St. Peter's Rooms, a church-owned building opposite the church. We candidates were all told to have a word with the Bishop, but I held back. He was surrounded by so many people, I didn't want to appear pushy. I did want to speak to him and tell him how Jesus had changed my life so wonderfully. But I never did. At that time I had not yet come to accept that Richard regarded himself as no more special or important to God than I was. I felt inferior to this man in such rich clothing. I had a lot to learn.

Some were going on to further celebrations at their homes afterwards. When I thought about it, I realised that in the eyes of the Christian this event was probably more important than that of a baby's christening. The public declaration of giving one's life to Christ was certainly good reason for celebrating. But Mike and I had arranged

105

nothing so we went to the local pub for a drink or two and then went home to relieve the baby-sitter. End of confirmation.

I've not seen many candidates from my confirmation since the service. The only one I do see regularly is Sue Lindley. She has been my prayer partner ever since. We meet regularly once a fortnight, have a couple of hours together, talking, laughing, crying, praying. It's been a valuable source of Christian contact. I know that I can trust her completely with everything. She's been a great sister in Christ to me. God was very clever when He put us on the same confirmation course.

On Wednesday 25th November at 7.00 p.m. we had our first encounter with our social worker, a very nice person. I'll give her the name of Joanne. She is extremely pretty and lovely with it. Joanne greeted us with a big beaming smile and I knew straight away that I'd be able to confide in her. I could identify with her. I was so pleased, particularly as I'd envisaged the arrival on our doorstep of a duffel coated, 2 CV-driving, short haired, no make-up, checked scarf, vegetarian, friends-of-the-earth frump. Television has a lot to answer for! But no, we had beautiful, long-haired Joanne.

Joanne explained to us the adoption process. It was a pretty lengthy and quite daunting one. It consisted of ten group sessions to be held with other hopeful adoptive couples, to discuss a wide range of topics. In addition, Joanne was to meet with us at our home for follow-up discussions from the group sessions and to conjure up a more intimate picture of the two of us. Then both she and the leader of the group sessions would write reports, which would be presented to a panel of social workers who would, hopefully, give us the official stamp of approval. Then we would wait for a child to be placed with us, on the understanding that there might never be one who would suit us or our family situation. Joanne also explained to us that the "fussier" we were about the age and sex of the child we would hope to adopt, the greater would be the probability of us ending up without a child. I said quite firmly that I wanted a daughter, preferably a young girl, no older than two years of age. Joanne made it quite clear to us that the chances of us getting a daughter under two were pretty slim. She informed us about the numbers of adoptive children available, producing pages of statistics. There were very few young girls in our age category.

So that was the score. Did we feel that we'd like her to start an official application for us? Well, I didn't feel all that enthusiastic, but I knew that Mike was keen to explore it all, so we agreed. There was no harm in starting the ball rolling. It would make Mike happy. But at that time I didn't feel any positive vibes about it. Besides, God was going to tell me in a few weeks time that I'd be O.K. to get pregnant.

Three months, to the day, after Julie had said that prayer, I said to God, "Right then tell me what to do. Tell me to get pregnant and that everything will be all right. Go on, please." Now what was it Julie had said? "Write it clear across the skies so she can't miss your answer." "Right then, God, if You're going to write it clear across the sky, I'd better start looking at it." So I did. Every night when I put out the milk bottles, I'd stay outside and have a good look. The nights were clear and the stars were all visible. But no, the stars weren't spelling out "Dot, get pregnant." I couldn't see any words, just stars. "Come on please, God, tell me to get pregnant and then it'll all be all right." By the end of the week I was getting a bit demoralised by not getting an answer. Mind you, I must confess that I had been looking for only one answer. Perhaps if God had spelled out "Dot, adopt," I would have dismissed it as my imagination and carried on with this almost obsessive desire to be pregnant.

Sunday came. I went to church in the evening not really anticipating any revelation. I listened to the sermon. I don't remember what it was about, but I do remember that Graham said one word that somehow registered within the dark recesses of my brain, and was stored there for future reference.

I went home and did my usual Sunday evening routine - ironing. I put on the T.V. and flicked through the channels. There was a programme on one channel about adoption that held my attention for a few minutes, but I felt in the mood for a comedy and found one on another channel. When I'd finished the ironing, I sat down to read the Radio and T.V. Times. I found a most intriguing article about the programme on adoption.

That week Mike and I decided to go out for a drink. So I dug out my baby-sitting list and started ringing round. It had been organised by a Mum who had a child at Sam's nursery school. There were about thirty Mums on the list. When I joined I was given 16 "tokens" which represented one hour each and I gave out the appropriate number of tokens for the hours I'd left the baby-sitter in charge. It was one extra token on

Fridays, Saturdays and Sundays, and double tokens after midnight. It was a good system. I chose someone I'd recently come to know, but not all that well. She came round and was sympathetically asking me what our plans for a future baby were. I told her that we didn't know, but that we had a choice of three options; One - me getting pregnant, which Mike didn't fancy. Two - me not getting pregnant, which I didn't fancy. Three - adoption, which Mike fancied but I didn't.

She hesitated, "You know my son..... well he's adopted."

"Is he really? Well, I'd never have guessed it. He looks just like you!" Mike and I went out and had a nice evening. I didn't think any more about what she'd said. I was still waiting for God to tell me to become pregnant.

On Sunday I went again to church. And I listened to the sermon. Again, one word seemed to register with me. "Adopt". That was in last week's sermon, wasn't it? As I walked home, I suddenly stopped in my tracks. Just a minute. This word "adopt" seems to be cropping up a bit. Is somebody trying to tell me something? No, it can't be. I shrugged my shoulders. No. No, you don't really get prayers answered. You say them. You ask. But you don't actually get *answers*. And anyway it wasn't the answer I wanted. So, it can't be right. No, no. Impossible. And then I thought - but it's been in Graham's sermons twice, and there was that programme on T.V., and also that article, and then there was the baby-sitter. I wonder - is God giving me an answer? I went all tingly inside. Then I shrugged my shoulders again and said out loud "Well, God, I don't want to adopt. I want to get pregnant again and have my own baby. I don't want somebody else's child." Then I paused and thought hard. I can't talk to God like this. How dare I? I set my chin firmly. "If You want me to adopt, God, then can I have it again in next week's sermon, please."

I went home and told no one about it. I waited for the following Sunday. It was a long week. I sat in church almost daring Graham to say that word. " I don't want to hear it, God, I don't want to hear it." But Graham said it. Quite clearly. It was as if he'd said it with extra emphasis. Just for me. I walked home, grim faced. "But I don't want to, God. You're supposed to be telling me to get pregnant." It seemed strange to be having a conversation with God. Yet I knew that He was there, listening to me. I didn't doubt that for one minute. It was adding a whole new dimension to my faith. Mindboggling stuff. I'd never known that He was available for me to communicate with here on earth. I'd somehow imagined Him as some superior intellect, high up in the Heavens, far above me, way out of my reach. I couldn't see Him, but I knew that He was there. Walking on, I sighed and resigned myself to it all. "O.K., God, if that's what You want me to do, then I'll do it. I have no choice. But if You *really* do want me to adopt, then I'd like the word "adopt" to be in Graham's sermon just once more. Then I'll really believe that You're telling me to adopt".

It was another long week. And the word was in the sermon, yet again. Extra loud. Just for me. So that was it. No pregnancy for Dot. Well, Mike would be pleased. I wasn't.

It was Wednesday morning. Fellowship morning. "Well girls, I've had an answer about what to do about another child."

Julie looked at me most intently and asked expectantly, "What is the answer?"

"Someone out there is telling me most definitely to adopt. I've been amazed. But I've no doubts about it. None at all. It's incredible. I've always prayed - at school and in Sunday School and in Church. But I've never had a real answer before. Or even expected one. Why was I never told that God can actually give you an answer?"

My Christian friends made no comment.

"Coming back to the question in hand, Dot," said Julie, "What are you going to do now? You asked God for an answer. He's given you one. Now what are you going to do with it?"

I looked at Julie quizzically - "You mean I have a choice? I thought that you had to do what God tells you to do. Fullstop." I know that my religious education had been lacking in some most vital areas, but one thing I did know was that, if God told anyone to do something then, my goodness, they did it. If they didn't then something pretty horrendous usually happened to them, either whilst they were still alive or after they died when they were condemned to everlasting Hell. How could Julie think that I could possibly consider not obeying God? I shuddered, thinking of the consequences.

I had already weighed it all up before I went to the meeting. Of course I was going to go along the road of adoption. Here was God telling me to do so. If I became pregnant, or tried to, I would not necessarily end up with a child - I'd already learned that one. But here was a definite direction from God, Himself! He wouldn't be telling me to adopt if I wasn't going to end up with an adopted child. God didn't work any other way.

God is love. He loves me. He wants to help me. And He was telling me to adopt. So it would be. I'd get a child by this route. I was beginning to feel extremely positive about adopting a child, because God, Himself, had told me to do so. After all, the two specialists at the hospitals had been poles apart in their advice. Mike and I had likewise been poles apart. But now - well God was telling me very simply, gently and firmly that the way forward was to adopt. I'd asked Him to change His mind, but He hadn't. And I knew that He knows best.

"No, Julie, I'm going to do what God's told me to do. It's got to be the right thing." And they all prayed for me and for Mike and for Sam and for our adoption application.

That evening when Mike arrived home from work, I told him that God had answered my prayer and had told me to adopt. Mike merely commented that he was very pleased that he and God were of the same mind.

No comment.

It was February 1988, Sunday morning. I was in Church. I felt fine. Everything was going smoothly. We'd praised God and worshipped Him. The sermon had been super. Graham really is a gifted preacher. Then came the bombshell. Before Graham started the prayers he told us that he'd been asked to pray specifically for a member of the Baptist Church, Sharon, who had occasionally attended our services. She was pregnant with twins and had been rushed into hospital with complications. There was a fear that the babies might want to be born, but they were too small to survive. I knew this lady. She'd been at my antenatal class when I was pregnant with Lydia. She'd had a boy. And now she was pregnant again. With twins! And Graham was asking me to pray for her!

Tears sprang into my eyes. I couldn't pray for her. I just couldn't. I was filled with so much envy. All I could think of was that she was going to have twins and my womb was empty. So what that I was going to adopt a child? So what that this adoption procedure was a mere formality and that I would get a daughter, the daughter I'd always wanted? It all seemed irrelevant at that time. She was having twins. *I* wanted twins.

Graham started praying. I tried. I did try. But the tears came. I felt sick inside. Please, God, I want a baby in *my* womb. Don't misunderstand me. I didn't want any harm to happen to those babies, I really didn't. I was simply full of envy. I'd never felt such envy before. It just didn't seem fair.

110

Graham prayed for the mother and her babies. And in my mind, I did so very much want her to have two perfect babies, born at a safe time for them to survive and for Jesus' name to be glorified through it. And indeed, it was so. But my heart ached, and I cried and cried and cried. I hurt so much.

I had such a longing to be pregnant again. I'd so enjoyed being pregnant with Sam and Lydia. I know that some women have positively disliked being pregnant, have been ill and looked awful. But I was the opposite. I had thrived every day of my pregnancy. I'd loved wearing my maternity dresses and letting the world know that I had a baby growing inside me. I'd had a healthy glow, just like that of all the ladies in the glossy magazines. I'd looked the epitome of health and happiness. Was I never going to experience that joy again? If not then I needed some help to cope with it.

The service ended. I stood up to walk out. I tried to hide the fact that I'd been crying. But I wasn't making a very good job of it. I lasted until I arrived at the door. I shook hands with Graham and then I burst into tears. He kept hold of my hand.

"I'm sorry, Graham," I blurted out. " But I just couldn't pray for Sharon. I know I should have. I know I'm going to adopt, but she's got *two* babies growing inside her and I haven't got *any*." I felt so stupid standing there like a little child declaring to my vicar that I wanted what somebody else had got, but that was just how I felt. I couldn't get away from the fact. I felt stripped bare of my feelings yet again.

Graham was still holding my hand. "I could see that you were struggling there." He paused...."I'm sure God understands how you feel."

I quickly walked home. "I'm sorry, God. I'm sorry," I kept saying through my tears. "I really hope her babies are O.K. It's just that I'm not pregnant. That's all." I didn't "labour" over it too much with Mike. I couldn't see the point. He was happy enough with the adoption. The last thing he wanted was for me to be pregnant.

That weekend I was expecting to start my monthly period. I'd been extremely regular since Lydia's arrival - twenty eight days, spot on. Monday came, Tuesday, Wednesday, and no period. I felt a bit excited. Could I possibly be pregnant? Surely not, but I was late. I was on the pill, but I knew that it was not 100% safe. I had mixed feelings. Had God changed His mind? Had He taken pity on me after my confession in church the previous Sunday? Perhaps I'd imagined God's message telling me to adopt?

Mike realised that I was late. He looked worried. I joked with him and said that, if I were pregnant, it'd be all right this time. He begged to differ. Thursday came, no period. Mike started to look positively ill. I was thrilled. Friday came, still no period. Mike looked like he'd got a sackload of potatoes on his shoulders, weighing him down. Mike has never been one to slouch. He's 6ft 4 1/2ins tall and has always stood straight. But now he was round-shouldered and grey around the gills. He looked desperate. I was still on cloud nine about being pregnant again, not thinking about the possible consequences. But my joy was being shaken by such a physical deterioration in Mike's appearance.

By Saturday, a whole week late, I was convinced that I was pregnant. I now felt scared as I started to think of the consequences of another pregnancy - but happy. Mike looked as if he would burst into tears at any moment. He looked awful. He had no colour in his cheeks. He had bags under his eyes. He was stooping something chronic. Nothing I could say comforted him. He just didn't want me pregnant. He'd had enough of pregnancies.

I stopped thinking about my desire to be pregnant. I looked at Mike, who was so sad and miserable, and so obviously worn out with it all. I'd never seen him like this before. Through all our traumas with Lydia, and the subsequent pregnancy and miscarriage, he'd always had an air of confidence about him, an "I'll manage somehow" appearance. But it had gone. Completely. Perhaps I'd been wrapped up so much with my own self-pity in those earlier situations that I'd not taken the time to stand back and see how Mike was coping with it all. I was certainly noticing him now. He was at breaking point.

The following day I went to the loo.... and I'd started. I was horrified for a moment, and shed a few tears of self-pity. Then I thought how happy Mike would be. And he was. His eyes shone with joy, his shoulders seemed suddenly to go back, as if the sack of potatoes had been shrugged off. He was *so* delighted and, amazingly, I was delighted for him. I felt as if a big barrier between us had gone. My selfish desires for a pregnancy, which could have worn down our relationship, seemed to go. I was happy that I wasn't pregnant, for Mike's sake. And I wanted him to be happy.

I went to Church and when we were again asked to pray for Sharon and her babies, I could do so with honesty, without envy. I was content not to be pregnant, and happy to be adopting a child, the child that God had got lined up for me. A child that hadn't yet been born. She was still in her mother's womb. I left church filled with a great sense of peace. I didn't want to get pregnant. I'd changed. In one week my feelings had completely been turned around. God had worked a mini-miracle in me.

Later, with God's help, I was sterilised with no pangs of regret whatsoever. That longing, that obsession to be pregnant, had gone. It had to go, for my own good. God in His infinite wisdom had taken it away from me. Praise God.

CHAPTER ELEVEN

Majorca

It was Monday the 9th May, 1988. Life felt pretty good. We had now happily settled on adoption, and were going to Majorca, flying away to the sun. Bliss. What more could I ask for? Well I didn't want a seven and a half hour flight delay but we got one. Never mind, we got there in the end.

On the first day Sam was sick. We took him to the doctors to discover that he had German measles and tonsillitis. Poor Sam, poor us! We managed quite well despite Sam's illness. Mike stayed with him in the mornings, while I went out exploring the shops. In the afternoons Mike went off on long walks, exploring everything but the shops! Mike loves walking. After four days, Sam was allowed out. He'd had quite a good time, all things considered. You know how it is when children are ill. They get more "quality" time than they do otherwise. There was no television for him to watch, so it was reading and colouring and drawing. It was really nice. In a way, it was almost a blessing in disguise, because Mike and I were able to do our own thing.

Now, the reason I'm writing about our holiday in Majorca is that two major events happened there which were to dramatically change our lives. We'll take Mike first.

He'd been reading a book by David Watson called "Is Anyone There?" David was recognised as a great evangelist. Mike had been greatly affected by this book. It had, literally, spoken volumes to him about Christianity. Mike had been looking at the Christian message for about a year and had come to the conclusion that if God wanted him to make a commitment of his life to Jesus, then he'd better do it. Mike has always been one for doing what is right and proper. He finished reading the book. And one night, there in Majorca, whilst lying in his bed, he gave himself to Jesus. He asked Him to take charge of his life. He confessed to

114

me later that nothing startling happened to him as he made the prayer. It was to be when he was Confirmed, in the tiny Anglican church in Edwalton, three miles from Ruddington, that he had a spiritual experience which made him aware of the power of Jesus.

Mike didn't tell me about his commitment until a few weeks later. He wanted to get himself used to the idea that he was a Christian before letting me and other people know. I must admit I felt a bit hurt that he didn't tell me immediately but, fair enough, it was his decision.

Now it's my turn.

It was our last day on holiday. We decided to spend the day on the beach. It was a glorious day. I kept applying the suntan lotion to Sam, but I didn't bother about myself. I quite often find myself doing things for others but not for myself. It's something to do with self-worth, so I'm told. Anyway, I spent all day in the sun and loved it.

I felt all right until Mike, who's a marvellous cook, began to prepare the evening meal. I started to feel queasy. "Oh no," I thought, "I've not overdone it, have I? I thought I was O.K. Oh no, please, I don't want to be sick. I hate being sick." I wasn't going to tell Mike, because he'd tell me off. He'd kept asking me if I wanted some cream on. I wasn't going to let him know I was suffering. I wasn't going to let him say "I told you so."

I suffered, but managed to put Sam to bed, whilst occasionally taking a few deep breaths. I told Mike I wasn't very hungry, so just a small meal for me, thanks. I sat down to eat. This is when the headache starts, isn't it? When your body's telling you it's been abused and it doesn't like it. I ate my meal. All of it. My insides were saying, I don't really want this, you know. I knew that I was going to be sick. Oh, but I don't want to be sick. I hate being sick. It was no good. I stood up. My head began to spin. "I'm just going to the loo, Mike. I don't feel very well."

He looked up, suddenly. "What's the matter?"

"Oh, I don't know."

"Have you had too much sun?" he asked, accusingly.

"No, I don't think so." (Liar.)

I walked to the loo as gracefully as I could, my head spinning. I'd gone all cold and clammy, and beads of perspiration were pouring out of me. I shut the door. "Oh, please, God, I don't wanna be sick. I hate being sick." I knelt at the bowl. This was it. My stomach retched. I'd reached the point of no return. "Please, God, no, no."

Suddenly that feeling of being sick completely went. Ooer. I looked around. I couldn't understand it. What *had* happened?

I went over it all. I'd been about to be sick and I'd said "Please, God, don't let me be sick," and it had stopped. I was startled. I felt all goose-pimply. Was that it? Had God stopped me being sick? When I'd said "please, God," I wasn't actually talking to Him. I'd been sort of, well - blaspheming, I suppose. Yet here I was, on my knees, still "praying" to the bowl and I hadn't been sick. God had heard and answered me, even though I wasn't really talking to Him. How awesome!

I stood up. I felt fine. This didn't seem real. What was I going to say to Mike? I couldn't tell him that God had stopped me from being sick. He'd think I was mad. Perhaps I was. But I knew I wasn't. I had a wash and went to see Mike.

"Were you sick then?" Mike asked, looking a bit cross.

"No I wasn't."

"I told you to put some cream on you, didn't I?"

"Yes, you did."

As I lay in bed that night, I thought about what had happened. It had been so amazing. It must have been God's hand on me. "Thank You, God," I whispered and fell asleep.

The next morning, the first thing that sprang to mind was what had happened the night before. It seemed so incredible. Had God really stopped me from being sick? Amazing! I just lay there revelling in it all. It was such a wonderful feeling. To think that God had answered my "prayer" when I hadn't really been talking to Him. I just couldn't grasp it all. It was quite simply a miracle. And He'd done it. For me. To me. Thank you, God. I felt all tingly inside. And all goose-pimply again. He'd heard me. He'd answered me. He knew I hated being sick. And He'd stopped it for me. I gave a little whimper of happiness. He loves me. Thank You so very much, God.

I felt that I had to tell someone about what had happened. I didn't feel able to say anything to Mike, but I felt that I could tell Sam about it. It seemed ungrateful not to declare what God had done for me. It didn't seem right. So, after breakfast, I tried, as casually as possible, to tell Sam about it.

"You know last night Sam? Well, er.... I didn't feel very well. In fact I felt quite sick. I thought I was actually going to be sick. So I went to the loo to be sick, but said "Please, God, don't let me be sick," and do you know what Sam? I wasn't. The feeling went away. God made me better." I waited....

Sam looked up at me. "Really, Mum?" His eyes all wide.

"Yes, Sam. Isn't He clever?" I sort of looked at Mike, who was at the far side of the room. He looked at me with one of his "You surely don't expect me to believe that, do you?" looks. He made no comment. Well, it was over and done with now. I didn't bring the subject up again. Or anything else!

It was some time later, back home, that I mentioned it again. It was at a fellowship meeting one Wednesday morning in the Vicarage. I told the group what had happened. We were a mixed bunch of Christians and non-Christians. My dear friend, Alison, who was not at that time a Christian, laughed at me, put her arms around me and said, "I admire your faith, Dot, and for telling us, but you're mad."

The Christians there just smiled at me. Julie, who was leading the session, added to my story - "He didn't tell you off, did He, Dot? He didn't say "naughty girl, you should have put some cream on, you deserve to be sick, so be sick," He simply healed you, because He loves you. That's God for you."

When we had arrived home from our holiday, we were horrified to hear that a boy had been knocked down by a car and killed just two streets away from where we live. He was only nine years old, came from a responsible family and knew his road-safety code. In fact, he'd got top marks in his school's road safety quiz.

But he was dead. The whole village was shocked. My heart went out to his parents. How awful for them. I thought of Sam and of how precious he is to me. The thought of him being run over made me feel dreadful. He seemed extra precious to me now. It made me realise that I sometimes take Sam for granted, assuming that he'll always be there. That he's tough and sensible enough to look after himself. I really mustn't be like that.

The Sunday morning after we'd come back from our holiday I went to church. I was walking along the road on which the boy had been killed, thinking about him and his family. His poor mum had given birth to him, looked after him, nurtured him and taught him how to look after himself.

She must have been looking forward to seeing him grow up to be a fine young man. All that had now been taken away from her. He'd gone. How awful. Because I'd lost Lydia and had a growing son myself, I could personally identify with some of her grief.

How awful to have your son taken away from you without warning. Out of the blue. As I considered this, something hit me. It was so shocking that it made me stop in my tracks. I thought of God watching His Son playing, laughing and crying as a boy, and then growing up into manhood knowing, actually *knowing* that His Son was going to die at the age of 33. To die painfully, embarrassingly and naked, on a cross, with people jeering at Him. What pain, what anguish God must have felt at times, as He saw His Son so innocently growing up. How terribly sad for God, and yet He did it. To actually allow His Son to die in that way. Could I do it? Could I watching my son grow up if I knew that he'd have to go through such a terrible ordeal when he was 33 years old? I don't think I'd have had the guts to do it. I'd have to chicken out. Try to compromise, somehow. But God didn't. What a sacrifice. How it must have hurt God. I went into church and cried, recognising God's love for me in that sacrifice.

Before, during and after going to Majorca I was reading lots of Christian books. I found the events which had happened to their writers, the help Jesus had given them, absolutely fascinating. I could hardly take in what I was reading. Why hadn't I come across books like these before? I read about people asking God for sunshine when they went on holiday and getting it, people praying for money for a specific item and then suddenly getting the exact amount required, people praying for food and then discovering food parcels on their doorsteps, people praying for healing and being healed - and it all made sense to me. After all, He was the Creator of everything good in the world. Nothing is impossible for Him. I read about angels helping people in danger. Later on I talked to someone from my church who had indeed been saved from a life / death situation by two angels - how fantastic! I read so many wonderful testimonies. It was quite awe inspiring.

I was also reading my Bible daily. I tried to tackle one chapter in the New Testament per day. I'd been told that it was probably the best place to start. And so I began to read the world's number one best seller. It was such an eye-opener to me. It seemed so much more interesting than when I'd read it at school. I used the N.I.V. translation, which I'd bought from

118

the local Christian Charity Shop. It's a shop run by a group of Christians from all the three churches in the village. It's called the Honeycomb. They will take from you any article which is no longer of any use to you, and they will sell it in the shop. Clothes are a major item in the shop but there are often prams, toys, books, bric-a-brac and jewellery to be seen. It's a real Aladdin's cave. Clothes given which are not sold go to meet the needs of people who are desperate for clothes. Most of them go to a central sorting place in Yorkshire where they are graded, even the waste is used for industrial rags. Shoes are sent abroad and toys, too. They also sell Christian cards and books. It's a busy shop, and a good witness to the community. The profits are used to meet the needs and to relieve hardship and distress both locally and world wide.

I didn't realise it at the time, but because I was now filled with The Holy Spirit, God could communicate to me what He wanted me to see through His Word. Certain verses seemed, as it were, to stand out in bold print. They were so relevant to my understanding of God, of Jesus and of The Holy Spirit.

The first verse which spoke specially to me was in the book of Philippians, 4:6-7. "Do not be anxious about anything, but in everything, by prayer and petition, with thanksgiving, present your requests to God. And the peace of God, which transcends all understanding, will guard your hearts and your mind in Christ Jesus." So wasn't I supposed to worry about anything then? Nothing at all? Well, I never knew that! So it's wrong for me to worry. It's not what God wants me to do? Is it a sin then, I wondered? I thought hard and then told God I was sorry that I'd been worrying about things. That I wouldn't do it any more. Not that I was a great worrier. It's just that I did get unnecessarily concerned about some things. So I began to do what this verse said. As soon as I realised that I was worrying about anything, I'd stop myself in my tracks and say a prayer. "Please, God, I'm worried about such and such. Can You sort it out for me, please?" And it was sorted out. Great. Thank You, God.

I fell into the habit quite quickly and easily. Although my list seemed never-ending some days, it stopped me worrying. It was great! Sometimes, when I was merely annoyed about something, I'd try to turn it into a worry and throw it to God.

A super example of this happened during the summer of 1988. At the bottom of our short garden there is a row of trees. The birds would often gather there for a sit and a sing-song. A street away from us there is a grain mill, so lots of birds were around us, as I'm sure you can imagine. That didn't worry or annoy me. It was all quite nice. How rural! But what *did* annoy me was the fact that they kept performing their natural duties on my washing. Quite often when I put the washing out, something ended up having to be washed again because of bird droppings. Now I didn't object to the occasional bit of extra washing, but the birds seemed to have a preference for my sheets. I had to wash the sheets again and again, and quite often had to use the tumble drier. This bugged me because it was summer time. I didn't want to pay to dry my sheets. So I sat down and tried to turn this annoyance into a worry.

And I did. And then I prayed. "Please, God, You tell me not to worry about anything. Well I'm worried about my electricity bills being higher than they need be. Lord God Almighty, Creator of those birds which come into my garden, could You please tell them not to perform all over my washing any more, please, God. Thank You, God. I ask all this in Jesus' name. Amen." And they stopped doing it on my washing, praise God.

Applying these verses in Scripture also helped me on those days when Mike was late home from work. Much of his work has included travelling, both in this country and abroad. I used to hate it when he arrived home later than planned. I'd try and keep calm, thinking that he'd probably got stuck in a traffic jam, or his appointment had run late, but I'd start worrying. He would sometimes come home when I was all tensed up, and instead of greeting him with a cheerful smile, I'd virtually shout at him in relief. I know of other wives who are like that. Anyway, I now started praying for him instead of worrying. "Please, God, bring Mike home safely. Protect him with angels, guide his path, give him the wisdom to know which roads to avoid and give me peace in all this. Protect him from the enemy." It's now a standing joke with us that when Mike's late home, and I greet him with a smile, he'll say something like, "Well I suppose you weren't worried about me being out in that awful weather, were you? I suppose you've been perfectly happy here whilst I've been driving in foul conditions. You've been praying again, haven't you?" It is *so* nice being a born again Christian!

That was dealing with worries on a personal scale. However, on a world scale also, Jesus has given me a great peace when I've started worrying about events which I've seen on the news. On some issues I've actually seen a tremendous answer to my prayer for help, on others I'm still praying them through, asking the Lord Jesus to guide me in how to pray for His hurting children. I can see now how He has made me worry about certain issues, so that He can use me for intercession. Here I'd like to tell you about two occasions when He has moved me to pray about certain happenings and the end result.

The first was when a seven year old girl, Gemma, was snatched from a caravan whilst asleep. Her parents were asleep in the next bedroom. It was August 1990 and the weather was hot. It was the obvious thing to do, to leave the window open. The kidnapper had simply reached through the window and grabbed her. The camp-site was shocked to the core that someone could kidnap a seven year old girl so easily. I watched the news and started to panic for her, for her safety, for her life, for fear of sexual abuse. I thought of my reactions if that should happen to my own child. Suddenly I realised that I was worrying about Gemma. Something clicked inside me, reminding me that I'm a Christian. I don't worry, do I? I give it to God. So I did just that.

I don't know how many times I prayed for her. I just knew that one prayer wasn't enough. I prayed and prayed. I couldn't get her off my mind. I wasn't at peace. I needed to keep on praying. I prayed God's protection on her, and that He might be able to speak to the man and prevent him from killing her. I prayed that she died at God's timing and not this man's timing. Jesus also touched Mike to pray for Gemma. On the Tuesday after Gemma's kidnapping, Mike went to Scarborough on a business trip. On his way back home he felt he'd like to pop into Beverley Minster. He'd never been inside it. Once there he felt moved to pray for Gemma. Imagine our joy and relief to hear that she was found safe and well. Oh, hallelujah! Praise God.

That summer also, a young woman had walked into a London hospital and walked out with a new-born baby. The natural mother appeared on television begging the kidnapper to bring her child back. It was heartbreaking to see this new mother filled with such turmoil. How would I have reacted if Sam had been taken away? She looked so frightened, so worried. Yet again Jesus "burdened" me to keep on praying for the baby's safety, claiming also that the kidnapper be protected from exploitation by the spiritual forces of evil. I don't know how many Christians God moved to pray for protection for that baby and the kidnapper, and also for Gemma and her kidnapper. Tens, twenties, hundreds, thousands maybe, perhaps only a handful. I only know that it was so thrilling to hear on the news that the child had been returned unharmed to the baby's natural mother. Praise God.

I remember the worrying time we had when Mike seemed to be working ridiculously long hours for a bus and coach manufacturer. Mike was really struggling with his boss. The firm was going through a really bad patch and his boss was giving everybody a hard time. He was in the habit of losing his temper and getting so agitated that his feet literally left the ground! Mike and I prayed for God to intervene. He certainly did, but not in the way we had expected. God is certainly a God of surprises. I'd hoped, and indeed prayed, that perhaps his boss might be moved to the other works' site, or perhaps Mike would. Imagine my shock when Mike walked in from work to tell me that his job had been made redundant. I was in a daze. Surely not, God, surely You've got it wrong? Mike's not supposed to lose his job. He's supposed to get promoted away from his boss. Are You sure You've got it right? It took me until lunchtime the next day to pull myself together and start do something positive, i.e., pray. Mike was amazingly at peace about it all. Euphoric in fact. He was away from his boss! *His* prayer had been answered! He celebrated his first day of being unemployed by going for a walk in Derbyshire. He climbed to the top of a big hill, sat, gazed at the beauty of God's creation displayed infront of him, read his Bible and was so very, very happy with his lot. In his Bible reading he came across the verse which says that God looks after His children, and Mike just had this total confidence that we'd be O.K. And we were, praise God.

Another occasion springs to mind when money was quite tight. Mike had moved on to a salesman's job that paid him commission on each order. The basic salary was quite low but he had been quite positive about being able to sell specialised machines. However, the orders failed to materialise. We needed some more money. I and my prayer partner, Sue, asked God to bless Mike with an order. He got one, which incidentally was the biggest single order that his company had ever had. Nice one, God. That's what I like about God. When He decides to do something, He does it with style! Then we came to the wilderness period. No further orders. For weeks, months. Help us please, God! Please bless Mike with another big order. No order. No money. Where are You, God, in all this?

At that time I was going to a monthly "discipleship" meeting organised by the Christian Centre in Talbot Street, Nottingham. It's a big well-organised church with some excellent courses. Upon leaving one meeting I picked up a leaflet from each of the piles of leaflets in the reception area. When I arrived home I gave them to Mike. Perhaps he'd find something interesting in them. A while later, he asked me to look at an advert in one of the leaflets. It was for a part-time French teacher's post at the King's School, a Christian school which the Christian Centre supported, one to two days per week. At first I was horrified. Me! Work! I didn't want to. I was too busy to work. Surely God didn't want me to go back to work!? Couldn't He just provide Mike with a big order and solve the financial problem that way? I prayed about it. I acknowledged that the right thing for me to do was to apply for the job and then see what happened. I had to apply. I had to open the door. God would shut it for me if that was His will. So I applied. And prayed for God to shut the door. Because I didn't want a permanent part-time job.

I'd been doing enough supply work in the local comprehensives schools to manage reasonably well financially. I'd quite liked the flexibility of doing such occasional work. I liked being able to avoid work on a certain day because I'd prearranged something. I liked not being tied down. I must confess, though, that I'd had some bad days recently doing my supply teaching. When you're a French teacher and someone asks you to take a biology class, or a woodwork class, or a drama class, you feel as if you're not helping the children at all, but pocketing the money for a poor days work. I knew that these children and myself were not getting a good deal. So, I prayed. Then I was invited to go and look around the school. So I prayed some more, and went. I met the Headteacher, Rob Southey, who had an informal "chat" with me, in which I told him virtually my whole life story. I felt quite exhausted. He gave me some very comforting words to encourage me regarding my sadness at the damage done to Sam.

I was given a guided tour of the school. It was situated in the upstairs area of the Christian Centre. An entire floor was given over to the school. The children all looked happy enough. The teachers all seemed very friendly. I'd never seen a set-up like it, though. The class areas were separated by partitions. I was used to teaching in a classroom, separate from all other classes. I wondered if I'd be able to manage a language lesson in such circumstances. I was assured that Liz, the other language teacher, didn't seem to have a problem with this. I was invited to go and see a school assembly. And it was just absolutely wonderful. The assembly was all about Jesus. And we sang to Jesus. Some children and staff had their arms raised in worship to Jesus. We heard a girl talking about how Jesus had changed her life. She had recently returned from a school trip to a Horizons Christian Outward Bound Centre in Wales, and had had a marvellous time there. We prayed to Jesus. Now that's what I call a Christian assembly!

Rob said he'd like me to go for an interview with two of the church elders. So I went home, said my prayers again, and waited to be called to interview. I was meanwhile asking my fellow Christians to pray that I would only get the job if God wanted me to. So they were all praying for me that the Lord's will be done, and I was asking Him to close the door, because surely I was meant to be available to go and have cups of coffee and a chat with people who needed God's help.

I went to the interview. There were two people, one man and one woman. "Right then, let's get on with the interview then. Let's pray," said the man, who'd introduced himself as Mike Bussell. What a lovely start to an interview, I thought. And as he prayed I felt a lovely warmth go through me. I knew that Jesus was there with me. I knew that His will would be done. I felt such an inner peace. It was wonderful. At the end of the interview Mike concluded that he'd not felt checked in his spirit by any of my answers, and the lady was of the same opinion. I was told that I would hear from them within a few days whether it was right to offer me the job. He added that the Lord might have something else for me to do. I went away from the interview praying that God would tell them very clearly whether they were to offer me a post there or not. I didn't want to have to make any decision. I wanted God to do all the decision making. That way I wouldn't get it wrong. A letter arrived. It invited me to accept the post of part-time French teacher at the King's School. After much soul searching I accepted the job. And do you know, it's been the most wonderful part-time job!

Mind you, it hasn't been a bed of roses. For a start, when I accepted the job, I was told that the Christian Centre had given the King's School notice to quit. The Centre was growing and needed the floor space. Rob didn't know where we were going to. He'd appreciate my prayers in this matter. So I had a job, but nowhere to teach! I had to laugh about it. This job was becoming more fascinating by the minute! At the eleventh hour a suitable building was found, St Faith's Church, in the Meadows district of the City. I was asked to bring a duster and some rubber gloves for the first day of term. The whole church needed cleaning and kitting out for teaching. So I turned up on the first day to find staff and parents all working together at trying to make this old unused church into a school. I was given the job of sanding down some old wooden chairs that had been donated. I could hardly believe that I was doing such a job. This is novel, I thought. I was used to teachers doing the teaching and cleaners doing the cleaning. Not so at this school. It's not like being employed by the County Council!

In my first year there, my class room was a portacabin round the back of the church. I could make as much or as little noise as I wanted to. The portacabins have now gone. There no longer is a Modern Language room. We've gained the building which was formerly the Vicarage, which we now call the Annexe, but the number of children in the school has grown. The language staff wander from one available room to another. I'm really longing for the realisation of a verse of scripture given to the school. "He is wooing us from the jaws of distress to a spacious place free from restriction, to the comfort of your table laden with choice food." (Job 36:16) As I said to Liz, I'll be happy just to get a table, never mind it being laden with choice food! Seriously though, the school is now bursting at the seams. We do need to move to a bigger building, but how, when and where, we do not know. So if you know of anybody who's got a potential school building going spare.... Let it be soon, please, God.

I'm told to pray for my children, pray for my salary, pray for equipment. I have no yearly budget, not like I was used to in secular education. The first time that I went to see Rob for some money for books, he told me that there was no money, that I was to go back to the class who needed the books and to pray for God to provide us with the books. I was absolutely amazed. Pray for some French text books! I'd never heard of anything like it before. I went back to my class and we dutifully prayed. Or rather the children did. I told them that we had nearly finished book one of the course and we would soon require twenty copies of book two. The children had no problem with my request for prayer. I did! They were obviously used to looking to God to supply their needs. I wasn't but I was learning fast!

It was about a week before I needed the books. I was feeling a bit desperate about them. My son was in his last year at South Wilford Endowed Junior School. I was in the process of looking at the local secondary schools, trying to work out which was the right school for him. My village is most fortunate to be surrounded by several excellent secondary schools. I'd done some supply teaching at most of them and had come to the conclusion that they all had their strengths and their weaknesses, that I was really splitting hairs about any one being "better" than any other. I decided to go to each of their open evenings in the belief that God would show me clearly which one was the right one for Sam. At the first school, which incidentally was not the one God told me to send Sam to, I had a conversation with the Head of Modern Languages. She was telling me about her new course books, the latest arrival on the language scene. She was very pleased with them. I asked her what course she had been using before. It was the course The King's School was using. My heart beat fast. Could I have her old books, please? I offered her 50 pence per book. She said yes, they would only be collecting dust in a cupboard somewhere. I was ecstatic. I went and told Rob what had happened, I told my class, I told my Christian friends. I thought it was wonderful. Those books were normally £7.50 each. What would have normally cost the school £150 had only cost £10. What an answer to prayer! Praise God. I did ask God why couldn't the King's School have this super new course, why did we have to make do with an older course? He gave me the answer that the old course would still get the good results. That's what mattered.

It was May 1988. I was sitting in a consulting room in the Queen's Medical Centre. Across from me were three male hospital officials. I was here to enquire whether I could be approved for sterilisation. We'd be "looked upon more favourably" by the adoption panel if one of us had been sterilised. Mike and I had discussed the subject fully and concluded that it was probably more practical for me to be sterilised than Mike. My body was obviously not very good at producing babies. I was the logical "volunteer" for the operation. The main spokesman looked at my file with interest and was friendly and "approachable". He listened most sympathetically as I told him about Sam and Lydia, and the miscarriage, and our application to adopt a child. I could tell that he was genuinely interested. He didn't talk to the other two men, so I assumed that they were

126

both students. "Did he think I could be put on the waiting list for the operation," I asked him.

He smiled kindly. "Well, I agree with you that you've had a rough time and that most probably the sensible thing to do is to adopt. But, I think I'd like to wait until you've been approved by the adoption panel before we perform the operation."

I was stunned. "But you don't seem to understand. If I'm sterilised now, then it will be one more thing in our favour to present to the adoption panel. In fact, they actually like it when one parent is sterile. That way there's no danger of the mother becoming pregnant once she's been given an adoptive child."

"I can appreciate that," he said gently, "but what if they didn't accept you for adoption, and we'd sterilised you. You'd have burned all your boats then. No. Come back once you've been accepted and then I'll sign the consent form for you."

I looked across at them. Everything in me wanted to say - but you don't understand. I *shall* be approved. We *shall* adopt. And there's a lot more too if you'd care to listen. But I didn't. It was three against one. Though with hindsight it was four against three. I had three others on my side of the table. But I lacked the courage to say anything. I politely left the room, and went home bitterly disappointed with my lack of boldness rather than anything else. God might have wanted me to speak to those three about Him, and I'd failed Him. And I'd failed me, too.

Suddenly it dawned on me that the refusal for sterilisation wouldn't be a stumbling block to our application for adoption. Nothing would be. God had shown me clearly that adoption was the way forward. So nothing could stop it from happening. I think that I was simply shocked that the doctor had said "No", when I'd been expecting him to say "Yes". Ah, well as it says in Isaiah 55:8-9 " For my thoughts are not your thoughts, neither are your ways my ways," declares the Lord. "As the heavens are higher than the earth, so are my ways higher than your ways and my thoughts than your thoughts."

As it turned out, I was sterilised in June 1989, *after* our approval for adoption.

CHAPTER TWELVE

Jesus Heals

It was a Sunday morning in September 1988 and I woke up feeling fine. It was my turn to teach at Junior Church. I was sharing my group with Judith, two weeks on and two weeks off. She and her husband, Hugh, were on holiday in the Himalayas, walking and climbing. I had a cup of tea in bed and then went to get washed. Half way through getting washed I started to feel queasy. I thought I'd sit on the loo. I knew that there was a sickness and diarrhoea bug going round, I hoped I hadn't got it.

Anyway, I sat there and, sure enough, I'd got diarrhoea. Then, suddenly, my head started spinning. Oh no! I thought, I'm going to be sick! I hate being sick. I didn't dare get off the loo. I needed a bucket or something. I shouted to Sam and he passed me the kiddies' step that he used to have in the bathroom to stand on when he needed a wash. I was there with the step on my knees, feeling as if I was going to throw up. I was cold, clammy and sweaty, and thought, "I'm not going to be able to do Junior Church. Someone else will have to do it." And then I remembered that Judith couldn't do it because she was in the Himalayas. But we had to have a leader there.

"It's no good," I thought, "I'll just have to get better." Suddenly I was reminded of Majorca. God had stopped me from being sick there. I needed to pray. What do I pray? I knew that there was no way that I could concentrate on a "meaningful" prayer. I was ill. I was suddenly reminded of a conversation I'd had a few weeks previously with Sylvia Sanderson, when she told me how she'd managed, at long last, to swim a width of the local swimming pool. She'd said that, all the time she was swimming, she'd been praying "Jesus saves, Jesus saves." So I sat there on the loo praying "Jesus saves", which soon turned to " Jesus heals". I said it over and over again. "Jesus heals. Jesus heals. Jesus heals."

Mike knocked on the bathroom door. "Are you all right, Dot?" "Yes," I groaned. "I'm just ill. I'll be O.K. soon. I'm asking Jesus to heal me. It's all right. Go back to bed."

"You're asking Jesus to heal you?..." There was a pause. "I'll go back to bed. Shout if you need me."

"Jesus heals. Jesus heals. Please God, I don't want to be sick. Please don't let me be sick. Please." The diarrhoea stopped. And my head stopped spinning. The cold sweat went. I was O.K. I'd been healed. Jesus had healed me. "Thank You, Jesus."

I went and taught my Junior Church group. I told the children about Jesus having healed me that morning. I thought that it was amazing how God had been able to remind me of so much during such a traumatic time. Talk about Holy Inspiration!

Now I'd experienced the tremendous healing power of Jesus, my attitude towards illnesses in my household had a complete turn-around. Sam was prone to tonsillitis and I was used to taking him to the doctors for antibiotics. But I thought, "Why should I? Why not simply ask Jesus to heal him?" So I did and the results often amazed me. I'm not saying that I stopped taking him to the doctors. Not at all. But my initial reaction of "Sam's ill - I'll 'phone the doctor," totally disappeared. Now it was - "Sam's ill, I'll ask Jesus to heal him." I don't know why He didn't do it every time, but when He didn't, I'd take Sam to the doctors and get some antibiotics. I never discovered any pattern to the healing. Sam was always healed and that was what mattered. I've never had any hang-ups about not being able to solve that mystery. God gave the doctors their brains, anyway. It's up to Him whether He chooses to heal people through doctors or not.

Thursday, 16th February 1989 arrived. Was it really fifteen months since we had had our first meeting with Joanne? It seemed like almost yesterday that she'd explained to us the intricacies of the adoption process. We'd had our group meetings with other hopeful "parents". We'd had our own private sessions with Joanne, so that we could both bare our souls to her without feeling inhibited by our partner. Not that I felt in any way restricted by Mike's presence. It was all part of the adoption procedure. And today was 'D' day. It was a lovely, sunny day. It was school half term, so Sam was at home with me. I woke up tingling, aware that this was going to be a very special day. I went into our sun-filled bathroom, praising God and thanking Him for the sun, for the trees, for the flowers, for all the things I knew He'd made. For the bugs in my garden, for spiders, for ants, for the birds and their songs. I thanked Him for Mike and for Sam, and I thanked Him for Jesus. I thanked Him for sending Jesus to die for me, for Mike, for Sam, for Joanne and for all the people on the adoption panel. And I asked Him that, through the power of His Holy Spirit, the adoption panel would today say a big "YES!" to our application. I asked God to give me peace and guidance for the day by filling me with His Holy Spirit. Then I went and dressed and set about my day.

Sam had a dental check up that morning. Everything was fine. That lunchtime I had arranged to have lunch with a friend, Jackie and her son, William, at the Lantern (a coffee shop run by Christians in our village). William decided not to come, so Sam, Jackie and I toddled off to spoil ourselves. Jackie was surprised that I wasn't tense about the panel meeting, especially when I'd told her that the panel had recently turned down a couple from the Clifton area, assigned to our social worker, much to everyone's amazement. "There's just no point in my being tense. How will that affect the panel's decision? God's told me to adopt. I've said my prayers this morning, so that's it as far as I'm concerned." I suppose to some people that might seem irresponsible and blasé, but I knew in my heart that I had indeed done everything in my *own* power to be acceptable to the panel. Now the rest had to be done by God's power. So, I was just leaving it all to Him.

That afternoon Sam and I went for a bike ride. Joanne had said that our application was scheduled for 3.00 p.m. and that it usually took the panel an hour to go through all the paperwork. We arrived home at 3.30 p.m. to find Linda Foster, a Christian from my church, and her daughter on our doorstep. Linda had two adopted children herself and had come round to find out if we had heard anything. They came in for coffee. I'd just put the kettle on when the 'phone rang.

"Hello, it's me - Joanne. Yes, it's all right, Dot. You've been approved. They only took half an hour."

I covered the mouthpiece and shouted through into the lounge. "We've been approved," to which Sam's immediate response was "Praise the Lord," and Linda burst out laughing. I said "Thanks and goodbye" to Joanne and went back to see Linda. "They only took half an hour to decide when usually it's an hour. Thank You, God."

Linda chuckled, "It was lovely to hear Sam say "Praise the Lord."" I gave Sam a big hug. "I'll just 'phone your Dad," which I did.

I could tell by his tone of voice that he was very moved. "Are you all right, Mike?"

"Yes, yes, I'm all right. I know it's different for you. You say that God told you to adopt, but He didn't tell me. What with other couples being turned down, I didn't want to have my hopes raised too high. But I'm O.K. Yes, I'm pleased. It's another hurdle passed."

Oh, Mike, you don't say much but when you do, you do. I knew it was hard for Mike to have me as a wife going around telling people "God's told us to adopt." What an absolute marvel he was, and still is. He's my big prop who's always there when I need human help. He's great. God was so clever when He arranged for Mike to move into the same house as me, me living in flat 4 and Mike moving into flat 5. Some talk about fate - what a load of rubbish. It's God's hand at work. Praise God. Thank you, God.

That evening, when Sam had gone to bed, Mike and I sat together on the settee, holding hands, so thrilled to be one stage nearer our dream. It was great. Life was wonderful.

Joanne had said she would 'phone and come and see us in the not too distant future. I was a really happy lady. I had a wonderful husband and son and I had Jesus in my life. And now I was going to have a daughter.

Everything was great. I felt on top of the world. But only for a while. A few days later, I was standing at the kitchen sink, thinking about our daughter-to-be, when an awful thought hit me and made my heart sink like a stone. God had told me to adopt, but perhaps the child He wanted me to adopt was not the type *I* wanted to. Perhaps she'd be in a wheelchair, or mentally handicapped? I started to panic. I didn't know what to do. If God told me He wanted me to have a child in a wheelchair, then I'd have to. I had no choice, but I didn't want to. What was I going to do? I needed some answers but I didn't feel that I could pray for an answer for myself. I was too involved. I'd probably not look for the answer God wanted to give me, because I'd not want to see it. I needed to ask someone whom I knew had visions. Caroline, the lady who'd had the vision of a girl looking at a present, and Julie, my house group leader, sprang to mind. Caroline, I knew, was a very busy person, so I invited Julie around for coffee.

Julie was the Christian who had originally prayed for God to tell me what to do about a baby. So I poured it all out to her. "Julie, what am I going to do? I want a little girl who's normal to be my daughter and I've just started panicking, thinking "Well, perhaps God doesn't want me to have a normal little girl." I know that there are lots of beautiful children who are in wheelchairs or who are mentally handicapped, and I know that they need to be adopted. But I personally don't want to, not if I have a choice. I want a little girl who's not physically or mentally handicapped. She doesn't have to be super-intelligent. If she wants to work on the cheese counter at 'Woollies' then that's fine by me. (When I was young it used to be a fairly standard joke that, if you weren't very bright, you could always get a job at Woolworths, on the cheese counter.) I want a daughter with whom I can share things, like walking down the street together. That's what I want. That's what I need."

"If God told you to adopt a child in a wheelchair, would you?" Julie asked, quietly.

"I'd have no choice, Julie. I have to obey God."

After Julie left, I prayed for peace of mind, and then dismissed it from my thoughts. I was taking Philippians 4:6-7 literally. I had to. "Do not be anxious about anything, but in everything, by prayer and petition, with thanksgiving, present your requests to God. And the peace of God, which transcends all understanding, will guard your hearts and your minds in Christ Jesus." Those wonderful verses in Scripture once again enabled me to feel at peace. Looking back I realise that, when I'd been panicking and had thought "I'll see Julie", it was God who had put that thought into my mind. Praise God.

It was over a week before I bumped into her again. I'd taken Sam to school and was walking home when I saw her walking in the opposite direction taking her son, David, to the nursery. "Hello, Julie, how are you?"

"Fine." She always greets everyone with a big beaming smile.

" Did you get any answer for me about the adoption?"

Her face suddenly went serious, "Yes I did."

"Well, what was it?"

"I can't really explain here. It's not the right place. I'll have to come and see you."

I didn't like the sound of this one little bit. "Why can't you tell me. It's not something awful is it?" I was starting to crumble inside.

"Oh no. I'm sure you're going to adopt. It's just that it can't be gone over in five minutes in the middle of the street."

"Why not?" I was thinking. "O.K., when can you come and see me?"

"I'll give you a ring once I get home from taking David."

So that was it. I walked home feeling absolutely awful. Tears kept welling up in my eyes and I kept trying to fight them back, but I'd give up and reach for a tissue. What now? What, or rather whom, did God want me to adopt? "Please, God, please. Just please." Poor Julie. What had I got her into? I rang her, rather than wait for her to ring me. "Well, Julie, when can we meet?"

"I'm ever so sorry, Dot, but I'm absolutely fully booked all day today." I couldn't believe it. "Surely you can squeeze me in somewhere, Julie."

"Dot, I'm sorry. I don't think I've had to say this to anyone, ever before, but I just can't fit you in at all. It'll have to be first thing tomorrow morning."

I just couldn't believe it. This was my daughter we were talking about. But there was nothing I could do. "O.K., Julie, tomorrow morning." I put the 'phone down and cried. "Please, God, please help me."

That lunch time I'd arranged to go to a "do" at the Lantern, the village's Christian cafe. A guest speaker, Robert Ferguson, who worshipped at the Talbot Street Christian Centre was, coming to give a talk. Before that there was a ploughman's lunch in the cafe. There I met two Mums from my teaching days at Fairham Comprehensive School in Clifton, which was a mile away from my village. It was so nice to see these people in such different circumstances. They were no longer Mums, but sisters. We talked about what their children were doing and about which church in Clifton they went to. I told them that I hadn't been a Christian when I taught their children, though I'd considered myself to be one.

After lunch, we all moved to the room upstairs ready for the talk. Robert began with several beautiful songs of worship, the ones that had always touched me. As we sang "As the deer pants for the water", tears welled up and I started to cry. I tried not to let anyone see, but I'd had to sit quite near the front and at an angle facing inwards, so that I could see the overhead projector. So really, almost everyone *could* see me. I went for the tissues again. I really should have had shares in Boots the Chemists! Through it all I was thinking, "What's Julie going to tell me tomorrow?"

Suddenly, Fiona McManus moved across next to me. Fiona is an absolutely super lady. She seems to have so few material things, yet so much of herself to give. She's the picture of humility. A truly tremendous Christian. She'd do anything for anyone. I've got a very long way to go to reach her standard of caring for others. And I'm sure she'd say she's got a long way to go before she could compare herself to Jesus' humility and care for others. Will I *ever* get there? Fiona put her arm around me. "I don't know what this is all about, Dot. But God wants me to tell you that He knows what is in your heart and that's what you'll get."

"Really? Honestly?" I thought. I couldn't say anything. I was too choked up. I just cried. Was I really going to get the little girl I so very much wanted? Thank You, God. Thank You. Thank You. Oh, I was so happy, so very happy. I just couldn't believe it. Now I was crying tears of joy. Everyone was singing and worshipping, I was crying and Fiona was cuddling me. I felt so happy that I thought my heart would burst. And I thought, "I bet these mothers from Clifton must think I'm mad. I'm the one who had responsibility for their children and here I am crying like a baby." But, somehow, it didn't matter.

I must now confess that I can't remember much of Robert's talk. I sat there in a daze with my mind in a spin. I kept repeating Fiona's words to myself - God knows what's in my heart and that's what I'll get. Wonderful! Tremendous!

After the formal talk, Gill, the Vicar's wife, grabbed hold of me and told me she was going to ask Robert to pray that I might speak in tongues. She knew I had a hang-up about it and thought Robert could help. You see, I'd read in so many Christian books how God had used people who could speak in tongues to intercede in certain situations, with such tremendous results that I wanted God to be able to use me in the same way, if He so wanted. I'd tried many times to pray in tongues, all to no avail. Yes, perhaps Robert could help me.

He sat and talked with me and Sue, my prayer partner. Two Christians from the local Baptist church joined us, because they also did not speak in tongues. Robert told us that *all* Spirit-filled Christians could speak in tongues if they wanted to. I said that I wanted to, but couldn't. He

134

told us how he had begun to speak in tongues. How he had accepted the gift by faith, and he had done it by saying, "Right, I shall now open my mouth and speak in tongues." And he had done so.

Now, I had felt a certain reluctance to speak in tongues, a holding back because I am a teacher of French. I am used to opening my mouth and speaking a "foreign" language, knowing exactly what I am saying, and being in *control* of it. The idea of speaking an unknown and incomprehensible language filled me with apprehension, if not awe. Yet I *did* so want to speak in tongues. I wanted everything that Christ wanted to offer me. I had a real thirst for anything and everything.

So Robert prayed for the four of us. Other Christians laid hands on us and, together with Robert, prayed in tongues. I tried hard not to listen to what they were saying, but somehow I couldn't. I was trying to translate what they were praying! Although I knew that one has to be blessed with the spiritual gift of the interpretation of tongues to know what people were saying, the language teacher in me was still hard at work.

A Christian, Jane, was trying to help me. "You're too tense. Relax. Just go la - la - la to a song". I tried, but I knew that I was trying too hard. Then a word did spring to mind. I didn't know if it had come from God or not. It seemed such a silly word. It was the word "shuggadum". I felt embarrassed saying it, and disappointed for the Christians who had been praying with me and for me. Robert was very kind and left me with instructions to keep on accepting the gift of tongues in faith. So I went home saying to myself "shuggadum, shuggadum" and feeling a right fool. Just as Satan wanted me to.

It was to be almost two years later that I, or should I say the Lord Jesus, broke through the barrier and I spoke fluently in tongues. I'll write about that later. I slept amazingly well that night, all things considered! I kept repeating what Fiona had said; "God knows what's in your heart and that's what you'll get." Whoopee!! Control yourself, woman!

The next day, March 2nd, Julie arrived. I could hardly control myself. I tried not to act as if I'd leapt to the door as soon as she'd rung the doorbell. I tried not to rush, taking her coat and hanging it up properly. I acted as if I'd not boiled the kettle three times and put the coffee and milk in the mugs already, so that we could sit down together as quickly as humanly possible to get started. But it was difficult! Eventually we began.

135

"First of all, Dot, I need to go over something you said to me last time. You said that you *need* a daughter. Do you *need* a daughter?"

I thought hard. "Well, I suppose not. I don't *need* a daughter. But I want one and God knows that I want one."

"Right. That's fine then, because as a Christian you don't need anyone, only Jesus."

I thought hard again. "Yes, O.K. Julie, "I nodded, "I can understand what you're saying. I'm sorry. I used the wrong word when I said I *needed* a daughter. What I should have said is that I *want* a daughter."

"Right, now the second thing is, you say you want a daughter. I've prayed for you and I feel that you *are* going to adopt, but I don't know if it's going to be a daughter. It could be a son. What would be your reaction to a son rather than a daughter?"

I looked and said rather matter-of-factly to her "But, Julie, we've only been approved for a little girl. They wouldn't offer us a boy. We said from day one that we wanted to adopt a little girl, up to two years old, and that's all we'll be offered."

"Oh," she said, "I didn't know that. I thought you'd just been approved to adopt a child."

"Oh, no, Julie. Sorry, didn't you know? No, it's a girl or nothing."

"Well," she said, with that smile spreading across her face, "You'll get a little girl then, I feel quite certain about that."

I started to relax. Things sounded quite positive.

"The third thing, Dot, is that I don't know what kind of child, sorry daughter, God wants you to adopt. I've prayed for you and all I've got for you is Psalm 37."

Psalm 37? I'd never heard of it. I think I only knew Psalm 23. Psalm 37..... what was in it for me? Shortly after that Julie left. Psalm 37. Psalm 37. I dashed upstairs to grab my Bible from my bedside cabinet. I frantically found the psalm, took a deep breath and started reading it, whilst silently panicking. It's quite a long psalm - 40 verses in all. But when I'd only reached verse 4 my heart started to get all excited and elated. Could it really be for me? I read quickly through the rest of the psalm and, not having felt any other verse make an impact on me, I began to re-read the psalm, but more slowly this time. And again, verse 4 made my heart go all a-flutter and I knew, without doubt, that that Verse 4 was for me. "Delight yourself in the Lord and he will give you the desires of your heart." Isn't that what Fiona had said to me? Delight. What does delight mean exactly? I wondered, was there a hidden catch?

I'm sorry, I still had so much caution added to my faith. I've been let down so many times in my life, and too often I'd apportioned part of the blame to God. (One has to blame someone, doesn't one?) To accept that God Himself was one hundred percent behind me still took a lot of getting used to. I reached for Mike's Good News version and turned to Psalm 37:4: "Seek your happiness in the Lord and He will give you your heart's desire." I started to cry yet again. I hope you're not getting fed up with all my crying. There's still a lot more crying to come! So I was going to get the child that was in my heart. And then I thought, "What child is in my heart?" Do I really know? And then I thought, "Does it really matter any more? God knows. Isn't that enough? Oh, I'm going to be so very happy with her. We're going to have a wonderful time together. I was so relieved. I felt emotionally elated and exhausted. I read through the psalm again. What a pretty awesome psalm, you must read it sometime if you haven't already done so.

I floated through the day on Cloud Nine. Is that biblical?! I couldn't wait to tell Mike about it. To say that he looked relieved would be an understatement. That night we went out with some friends for a drink. I was on a high, and although they weren't born-again Christians I wanted to tell them about everything, but I held back. I believed they would not have understood. That's one of the sad things about being a Christian, isn't it? When God's done something truly wonderful in your day, you can't tell your friends and family if they're not Christians, because they can't understand? Indeed some just don't want to know. It's been very hard at times to accept that, but I am gradually coming to terms with it.

A letter arrived from Social Services. It was very brief and to the point. It informed us that we had been successful in our application to be accepted as adoptive parents. It added that it did not, in any way, presume that there would be a child suitable for us to adopt. It was a really miserable letter. What could have been a joyful letter, was in fact, full of doom and gloom. I appreciate that Social Services have to be practical and not raise people's hopes too high. Thank goodness I knew that we did have a little girl somewhere who was "suitable". Thanks, God.

CHAPTER THIRTEEN

The Prophesy

It was Thursday 13th April 1988. I'd arranged to go and see Geoff Kelk at his home. Let me tell you a bit about Geoff. Geoff at that time was a very active man within the village community, in several areas of public interest. At that time he was Chairman of the village council. He was also the Chairman of the Governors at the local junior school where I was Diocesan School Governor. Geoff suffers badly from arthritis in his legs. He's had surgery on his knees several times and was a regular patient both at the now closed Harlow Wood specialist hospital near Mansfield, about 20 miles from Ruddington, and the Queen's Medical Centre (Nottingham's big teaching hospital).

I went to see him on an educational issue, but I was to come away with a far more personal matter completely thrown open. What happened at Geoff's bungalow was to fill me with wonder and awe again as to what God can do in one's life.

It was what happened after discussion of the educational issues that I recall vividly. Geoff is, at times, touched by the healing hand of Jesus. He feels the presence of a hand on his head and knows that it is Jesus touching him, healing him. He has felt that touch on several occasions. He says that the sensation starts on his head, then he feels a warmth going slowly throughout his whole body, leaving him with a feeling of total peace and contentment. How wonderful, to feel Jesus' hand healing you. What an experience. What a joy, a thrill that must be. Geoff told me that twice that week he had been touched in this way after praying with two other Christians from my church.

Geoff and I prayed for the school. We finished our prayers.

"It's happening again, Dot. It makes me feel all weak." And there, in front of me, was Geoff, totally overcome by Jesus' healing hand. He just

138

sat there in his chair and waited for the healing power to pass through him. I sat there absolutely awe-struck. It was (and I'm struggling here for words to describe my feelings) a sight that filled me with such wonder and elation. How wonderful for Geoff to be touched and blessed in this way, and for me to be in a room where Jesus was healing someone. I can now understand how the people in Jesus' time had to bow down and give their lives to Him, and acknowledge Him as the Messiah, the One sent by God, after they'd seen Him perform a miracle.

It was over. Geoff was sitting up. He decided to make a drink. Soon the kettle was boiling. "How's things with your adoption, Dot? What stage have you got to?"

"Well, we've now got official approval to adopt. They say that it'll probably be at least a year before we actually get a daughter. But, you know, Geoff, I must confess that I don't *feel* it'll be a year. I've had premature babies. Sam was eight weeks early and Lydia was ten weeks early, so I have a gut-feeling that this baby will be early too."

"Hmmm," he said, gazing out of the window, "It'll be before October."

I looked at him in amazement. "What *are* you talking about, Geoff? You don't know anything about the adoption. How can you possibly say "Before October?"

He just smiled, shrugged his shoulders, and laughed, "I don't know. It just came to me. Before October. Yes, that's when you'll get her."

I started to get a bit agitated. Had he gone mad? "But, Geoff, how can you know?" And then I stopped. My heart started to beat frantically. "Is this from the Lord, Geoff? Is this for me from the Lord?" My heartbeat was just about quadrupled here.

"I don't know. It must be," said Geoff, shrugging his shoulders again. "Before October." Then he paused. "But I can't guarantee that she will be white."

Here my heart started to slow down. I thought long and hard. "That can't be from the Lord, Geoff." I said, slowly and deliberately. "I'd adopt a black child if God told me to, but Social Services won't allow white parents to adopt non - white children, not nowadays. We've only been approved to adopt a white child. That *can't* be from the Lord." I was confused.

139

"No, I asked you that to see if you were racially prejudiced or not. You see, I can't stand racial prejudice in anyone. I was just checking for myself about you."

Geoff certainly had no need to concern himself with me on that score. I can look at anyone and acknowledge him or her as my brother or sister, my equal, and know that I am neither superior nor inferior to anyone else in any way. But that is as a result of being a born-again Christian. Previously however, I do believe that I was very much conditioned by television and the media to think that I was indeed superior to people of different races and cultures. I had been brought up on films where the white people had black slaves, where white cowboys killed red Indians, where British people ruled over Indians, where natives living in jungles were put across as being ignorant and barbaric, in need of being educated by a white person. I grew up seeing black people being refused entry into Great Britain, and white people being welcomed into other countries. I had been encouraged to think that to be British was something to be proud of, (we won the war, didn't we?) in such a way that I felt that perhaps all other nations were inferior to my own. Rule Britannia and all that! God, however has, by the power of the Holy Spirit now in me, been re-programming me! We're all equal in God's eyes, aren't we? Praise God.

"You'll get her before October." My heart soared. Really, God? So soon. Thank You. Thank You. I tried to have a reasonable chat with Geoff over our cup of coffee, but I wasn't really with him any more. I was with my daughter. Before October. Before October. I kept repeating it in my mind. I couldn't wait to get home to 'phone Mike and tell him.

Can you imagine it, when he heard the news? There's Mike at work and his wife 'phones him up to tell him she's been praying with a man whom he hardly knows, and this man has told his wife that they're going to get their adopted daughter before October, when Social Services have said that it would be next February at the earliest. What would you have said in Mike's position, "You're mad woman," or "Great" or what? He hesitated and said, "Well, I admire your faith, Dot. We'll see." I wonder if he managed to carry on with his work after that?

I was so excited. Before October. My mind raced ahead. I began to make plans. Well, I'm only human. Now, if it's before October, it will be September, so I won't be able to work in September. So I'd better let the schools know that I won't be available for supply teaching next term. And

140

that meant my night-school class as well. My Holiday French night-school class had been talking of perhaps doing a follow-on year. But I didn't feel I could do that now. Not if I was going to get my daughter. I didn't know how old she'd be, or if she'd need a lot of settling in, or be so insecure that she'd need me around for most of her waking hours, or if she'd need feeding early evening. I might have had a bad reaction from Sam and needed to be there at all times for *his sake*, not hers. There were so many unknown factors. The only facts that we did know were that she'd be a white girl, aged between nought and two. She was the little girl who was in my heart and she'd be here before October. What a combination! However, as it turned out, I could have carried on working with no problems, but I'm glad I didn't. You see, God had His hand on it all.

Whilst all this had been going on - our acceptance by the panel, Julie coming to see me, the Robert Ferguson talk and my meeting with Geoff - there had been certain goings on in Nottingham which had hit the National press and horrified a lot of people including me. It was the case of alleged Satanic activity by a large family in Nottingham. It was horrendous. Before my conversion I had always believed in my Bible stories and had accepted that Satan existed. But now I *knew* in my spirit that he was for real, and I was seeing how he was making some awful things happen in this world, by encouraging sinners to do some terrible things. I include myself here as a rescued and changing sinner, now turned saint. (I'm very pleased that the Bible declares all born-again Christians as saints, even though I don't feel like one at times!)

I knew that the children had been taken away from their families and were being placed for adoption. And I knew that these children needed help. And I also knew that the best type of human beings who could help in healing these children were Spirit-filled Christians. So the big question was, "Was there a little girl there whom God wanted us to adopt?" I must admit that I didn't know if it was right for my family or not. I talked it over with Mike and he agreed that it did seem a pretty horrendous thing to volunteer for, but it did need to be looked into. So I 'phoned Joanne and she said she'd look into it for us.

She 'phoned me soon after to say that there *was* a little girl in the age group we were considering, but did we know what we would be taking on? "No", I said, and she told me some of the things we could expect a child who had been involved in Satanic activity to do. Did I want to expose Sam to this? I thought hard. "No, I don't, but if God wants us to adopt such a child, then it would be right and God would equip us all to cope with it."

I left it with Joanne to approach the social workers who were involved in the case to see what happened next. And I prayed.

A few days later Joanne rang me back to say that we were not considered a suitable family because we lived too close to their home and there was a possibility I might bump into them if I ever went into Nottingham. I'd have to avoid going into the city for some time. In a way, I was relieved. I had been a bit frightened at the thought of taking on such a child because, at that time, I hadn't done much reading about Satan. Ignorance can be so dangerous at times. In this case it certainly was. Now I've "read up" on him and discovered Satan for who he really is, I'm not frightened of him at all. Indeed, I've learned that to be frightened of Satan is an un-Christian act. As a Christian, I've learned that I should only fear the wrath of God. Yet I have struggled with coming to terms with God's wrath. He has been gracious enough to wait patiently for me to be ready to understand His anger. I'll go into more detail about that in a later chapter. That's not to say that the activities of the Devil don't upset me. There's many a time when his actions have brought me to tears. When I look at what he or rather his "helpers" have done to my family and my friends, well my blood goes cold. And yet I respect him. I have to. The Bible tells me to. Before my conversion I had had rather silly pictures of the Devil in my mind. I saw him sitting on a fiery rock with a trident in his hand, with smoke and fire all around him. I think I can blame television for that. It does have a lot to answer for, doesn't it? And the books I used to read whilst an impressionable teenager had filled me with a fear of him. I'd read all the Dennis Wheatley books, e.g., "To the Devil a Daughter", "The Devil Rides Out" and found them fascinating. But now I knew that the Devil, as God created him, was once beautiful. The most beautiful angel in the heavenly realm. He was God's choice as leader of the angels. Whenever I think of the Devil, I picture him the way God created him. It reminds me of his position in the spiritual realm, under God's power. It gives me peace. I don't know what he looks like nowadays of course, but one of the most impressionable books I've read has been Frank Perretti's "This Present Darkness". I appreciate that it's fiction, not fact, but I thought it a brilliant book.

On two separate occasions, in April and June, Joanne came to see us. She wanted to talk to us about the possibility of adopting either of two girls whose life histories had been given to her. The system was such that our names were now circulated to Social Services departments throughout the county. If they had a little girl between nought and two on their books, they would consider contacting Joanne, if they felt that we might be suitable parents.

I'm going to combine the two children into one here to show you the questions which were put to us. This is to protect the two children. I'm also giving you here our reasons for saying "no" to them.

Question one: What would you feel about the possibility of your daughter being of mixed race and it not showing up initially?

My initial reaction was that it wouldn't matter. But then I thought about it more deeply. It might not be fair to her. She could be awfully confused. If the rest of your family is white it could perhaps create unnecessary tensions. Then again, I know of a white Christian couple who have adopted three black children, and what a marvellous job they've done with them. I considered Sam, thinking he might feel strange having a half-caste sister. I thought long and hard and realised that in my heart of hearts I wanted a white daughter, because I had a white son and a white husband, and I was white. Suddenly Psalm 37 came to mind. The little girl *in my heart* was white.

"No, Joanne, if I have the choice, I'd say no."

Question two: This concerned a girl with a medical problem. This child had, on occasions, held her breath and turned blue for no apparent reason. It had just happened.

Now, for Mike, this had conjured up pictures of Lydia and he didn't want to have a repeat performance. "I had enough of that at the hospital. I don't really want to have a little girl in this house doing it." Mike's reaction took me by surprise. I personally felt able to handle it in another daughter. However, Mike obviously felt most uneasy about this child. He had to feel one hundred per cent positive about the child we chose. So she couldn't be the one.

"No, Joanne, we don't want a daughter who turns blue."

Question three: What if you were offered a child and you couldn't be told anything at all about the father? He'd disappeared. He could be a mass-murderer for all you know. What would you feel about that?

143

Goodness me, Joanne. Whatever next? Now, what could be the worst scenario? Let's say he was a murderer, an absolute out and out crook. How would we feel about having a murderer's daughter? Well, I knew Jesus could cut her off from her past through prayer, as I'd read in my Bible. But God had said He knew what was in my heart and this picture that Joanne was painting was not what I had envisaged for myself. We discussed the implications and answered "No".

Question four: What would you say if the girl's mother was, say, a prostitute?

Oh, Joanne, my goodness. My initial reaction was no thank you very much. I didn't want a prostitute's daughter. And then I thought hard. Well, how do I tackle this one? I concluded that I would apply the same Bible texts as those concerning a father being a murderer, Matthew 18 verse 18 sprang to mind immediately. "I tell you the truth, whatever you bind on earth will be bound in heaven, and whatever you loose on earth will be loosed in heaven." And so what if she was a prostitute? There could have been terrible circumstances which had forced her into this "profession". She could have been a really super lady. I know one retired prostitute who is a very caring person. So what had seemed to be an awful question had, through discussion, produced a less negative reaction from me.

However, yet again I thought of Psalm 37. A prostitute's daughter was not what my heart wanted.

Question five: What if Mum and Dad were both of limited intelligence, had both needed to go to special schools?

The question of the parents' limited intelligence and special schooling didn't cause concern for Mike, but it did for me. Now I know that a Mum and a Dad of limited intelligence do not necessarily have a child with a low I.Q. I know, from personal experience in the teaching profession that some not-too-bright parents can have a genius and that some extremely bright parents can have a child who has an extremely low I.Q.. Yet something niggled me. I started to talk all round the houses about it. Would it be fair to Sam to have a sister with an extremely low I.Q.? Would she "fit in" with our lifestyle? It all had to be taken into account. Mike was surprised at my protests. He thought it would be nice to help a little girl grow up in a loving, caring home, knowing that, if she wasn't all that bright, it really didn't matter. I didn't know what I was panicking about, but warning bells were ringing. And then I thought of my Psalm 37 and stopped panicking.

"No, Joanne, that child's not for me."

Question six : What would you say to the possibility of your daughter having AIDS?

That's a good question, isn't it? Well, if I had a choice, I'm sure I'd say "No". I looked at Mike. How can you answer that? Could we take on such a child? I thought long and hard. As a Christian I knew I could ask Jesus to heal her, and He would equip us and the child to cope with her illness. Did God want us to adopt a child with AIDS? And then I thought of what He'd said. I'd get the little girl who was in my heart. *She* didn't have AIDS.

"No, Joanne. I don't think I'd willingly volunteer to have a daughter who had AIDS." Mike agreed with me insomuch as he felt that, if his daughter showed no traces of AIDS through initial tests, but it happened that some years later it was discovered that she had AIDS, then he'd accept it, just as a parent accepts it when their child suddenly becomes asthmatic or diabetic.

There was one more point which I'd like to mention here. In the literature we'd been given by social services I had read that some couples had said "Yes" to the first child whom they were approached about, in case they might not be offered another. Then years later, usually during the child's adolescence, big problems had erupted, ending sometimes in a total breakdown in relationship. It was the classic situation, a family argument, and the mother or father suddenly yelling at the child, "I always had my doubts as to whether we should adopt you, what with your background." Now I knew that there was a child for us somewhere in the system. She had our name stamped all over her. It was just a matter of finding her. So I never lost a moment's sleep wondering if we had done the wrong thing by saying "No" to these two girls. They weren't meant for us. I prayed God's help for these children to be adopted by the parents He had chosen. We were later informed that they had both been adopted. Praise God.

Life was going relatively well. We were waiting to hear from Joanne about a child. But it wasn't as if I was waiting anxiously by the 'phone. I wasn't thinking that, whenever it rang, this could be Joanne telling us about a child. I was totally at peace. Some people asked me if I was worried about whether we would get a child or not. I felt so confident, that I could say with total conviction, that there was no doubt whatsoever that we would get a daughter. I had actually told some people that I believed God had told me to adopt. Nobody was aghast at my story. I even told my story to a friend who is an atheist. He laughed, but could not deny that I felt that Somebody or Something was telling me to adopt.

I would often imagine what life would be like once I had my daughter. It made me feel really gooey inside. We were going to have such a lovely time.

One day, whilst at the kitchen sink, thinking about it all, it suddenly struck me. God had told me to adopt a child. One day I would have that child. And God knew, even at that very moment, which child it would be because He knows everything. He knew the colour of her hair and eyes, and who her parents were. And He was giving her to me to look after. And He'd be watching me. Watching me bringing her up. Suddenly I felt quite scared. He'd be watching me, every second of the day, seeing how I was looking after this child. What a responsibility I had. What an awesome task God had given to me. To look after this child. She was obviously a very special child. Goodness, I hoped I could do it.

A few days later, something else dawned on me. In God's eyes, everyone is special. And Sam was no less special than my future daughter. God wanted me to do just as good a job looking after Sam as He wanted me to do with this child He had lined up for me. I felt a real burden of responsibility put on me. Sam and my daughter, whoever she was, were both gifts from God. Without God I would have neither of them. And I had to bring them up as best I could, and I knew that I would be totally answerable to Jesus, come Judgement Day. I'd have to stand in front of Him and He'd judge how I'd brought up Sam and my daughter, God's gifts to me.

I suddenly felt quite sick inside. I must have done a million things wrong with Sam, and God had watched me doing them. I cringed, thinking of the times I'd been unreasonable with Sam, telling him off when he hadn't deserved it. I'd just been feeling in a bad, selfish mood and lashed out at him verbally. I know that I had the excuse of being depressed with the trauma of Lydia and the miscarriage. Even so, I'd not behaved as God would have liked me to. I'd not really looked on Sam in this light before. I'd considered him as mine. A product from *my* womb, made by

146

me and Mike. God hadn't had a look-in in my life until now. I'd never looked at it from this angle before. Oh help. All the times I'd thought that Sam was only answerable to Mike and me, that we had the final say in his upbringing, and that we could virtually do with him what we wanted. Suddenly I realised that I'd got it all wrong. Sam was a gift from God, God's child. I was the person chosen by God to look after him.

What could I do? Pray and ask for forgiveness? I was sorry for anything and everything that I had done that could have possibly been wrong in God's eyes. I named some things and asked God to help me bring His child up the way He wanted me to. I was a long time in prayer. I was frightened.

When I finally surfaced, I felt I'd moved a big step along the narrow Christian path. I would now be a better mother and person. I had to be. I felt quite drained by it all. To think that after we'd been approved by the adoption panel I'd joked about making for myself a badge that said "I'm a brilliant parent!", accepting that Social Services were pretty tough at vetting applicants!

A month passed by and we heard nothing from Joanne, but I was expectant. I was certain I was going to get my little girl before October. And I told friends so.

"You have to be careful, Dot, when another Christian tells you something and says it is from the Lord. There's been many an occasion when it has not been so," a close Christian friend advised me. I knew that she was trying to protect me, and I knew that she was wise to do so, but she couldn't have said anything to convince me that what Geoff had said to me was not from God. I *knew* it was. I was *so* excited!

CHAPTER FOURTEEN

The Answer

It was June, 1989. I was in hospital, to be sterilised. It's not a very complicated operation, so I wasn't very concerned about it. After what Mike, I and Sam had gone through at the Q.M.C. this was nothing to make a fuss over. And I most certainly wasn't going to worry about it! It was Sunday tea-time. I'd just spent an extremely pleasant afternoon at church, where one of our young couples had had their son christened that morning. We'd had a super "faith" lunch on the church lawn, i.e., everyone had brought something sweet and savoury, enough for one's own family and a bit extra for any visitors to the church, and pooled it. The sun had shone, and I was thoroughly relaxed. I had had to book myself in on the Sunday for Monday morning surgery. A nurse came to my bed with a writing pad and she proceeded to take down some of my particulars. These included all the usual stuff - name, address, age, family, occupation, etc. But there was one question which I would like to tell you about, because my answer was to greatly affect my life, in a most disarming way.

"Tell me about your hobbies, Dorothy."

"Well let me see now. I like baking, knitting, walking and of course there's the church."

"The church?"

"Yes, I'm a Christian, I'm very involved with the local church." Perhaps I'll get a chance here to tell her my story, I thought.

"What sort of things are you involved in?" she asked. "Coffee mornings? Fund raising?"

I was horrified. I couldn't think of anything I'd hate to be more involved in than coffee mornings or fund raising. "Oh, no. No! I....I...." I struggled to find the correct words to describe what role I played. "I'm ....I'm....er, an evangelist," I blurted out. An evangelist! Where on earth did

148

that word come from? "Yes, that's what I am. I'm an evangelist!" I sat back in amazement at what I'd said. An evangelist! Was I really an evangelist? Gosh! The nurse made no comment at what had appeared to me to have been quite an earth-shattering statement. She asked me a few more questions, and then left me to ponder over what I had said.

Me! An evangelist! Well I knew that I had a real longing in my heart to tell everyone about Jesus and what He'd done for me. I knew that I had a super story to tell. Had God made me an evangelist? Wow! I sat there thinking it all over. Dot Houghton, an evangelist! I suddenly felt very important. Too important, to be honest. Right then, God, I thought, bring them to me then. I'll tell them all about you.

I sat there, looking at the other three people sharing the ward with me. These'll do for starters, I thought. Let's get them converted. What is it they say? Fools rush in where angels fear to tread.... But nothing happened. Nothing. We talked about lots of things during my few days there but nothing Christian was ever discussed. I tried, I really tried to talk about Jesus, but they changed the subject every time. They were clearly uninterested in Jesus. And I prayed so hard, I really did. I really wanted to bring these people to their knees and ask Jesus into their lives. But absolutely nothing happened. And do you know what? I'd have been unbearable to be with if it had. At that time I was so full of pride at the thought of being an evangelist. It would have been to the glory of Dot rather than to the glory of God. How awful. How disgraceful.

When I was finally discharged and walking out of the hospital, I bumped into a lady I knew from my teaching days in Clifton. She and her daughter were visiting her young grandson who was recovering from an operation. Apparently, he had spent a lot of his young life in and out of the Q.M.C. We exchanged pleasantries. Perhaps these were the people God wanted me to evangelise to? I tried. But nothing. I said "Goodbye" to them and walked away bitterly disappointed that they hadn't been convicted by anything I'd said. I should have heard the warning bells then, I suppose, but I didn't. However, my ears were still resounding with "I'm an evangelist", so I wouldn't have heard them anyway.

That event was to dominate my way of life for quite a long time. I went round telling everyone who would give me the time of day about what Jesus had done for me. And none of them fell onto their knees and came to Christ. Because you see, I wasn't an evangelist, well not in the way that I then understood the word "evangelist". I had heard of evangelists like Billy Graham, chosen by God to be used to bring many people to a living faith in Jesus. I had very wrongly assumed that that was what God had chosen for me to do. I've since learned that an evangelist can be someone chosen by God to speak to Christians and non-Christians about the gospel. I was putting too much emphasis on talking to the non-Christians, indeed I was overdoing it, with a most negative result. I eventually realised that I was more of a demoraliser than an encourager. I was trying to evangelise to people whom God simply wanted me to tell my story, to encourage them on their journey of faith. A Christian did try to give me a big hint, but I didn't take it. Anne Saville used to be in charge of buying Christian books for the Honeycomb charity shop in the village. I asked her if she would get me a supply of booklets like the Norman Warren one I'd been given, to give out to people. She came back to me with a paperback entitled "How to explain your faith without losing your friends". I felt most taken aback, but didn't change my ways. I was after all an evangelist. I cringe even now when I think of some of those occasions when I'd tried to sell the gospel. Such lack of wisdom, gentleness and tact. Yet God has forgiven me each time. If you're one of the people to whom I've tried to "evangelise", please accept my most humble apologies. God has.

I don't believe for one minute that I'm not alone in trying to "evangelise" to people whom God doesn't want us to. Indeed, I've spoken to quite a few Christians who, once they've had their first encounter with Jesus, have driven their friends away through their desire to get them converted. Let's not be too hard on ourselves. Jesus, in the closing words of the gospel of Matthew, tells us to go and make disciples of all nations. It's just that God's timing and our timing aren't always at the same time. Wisdom, wisdom ....

I have to admit that gentleness has not been one of my prominent characteristics, but if I could perhaps expand here on the subject then you might see why. I had three elder brothers. Two were nine years older than me, and one eleven. I had no Mum. My Dad did not set an example of gentleness for me to copy. He was the man who spent all his time looking after our material needs. His hands were already full. I don't imagine that gentleness was on his list of priorities. Would it have been on yours if you were him? His gentleness had probably been knocked out of him once my

Mum had died. Before he had met my Mum, when he was young, he'd had to be tough. His father had died when he was quite young, and he had been left with five brothers and his mother to look after. I'm told of the times he went scavenging and poaching for food during the Depression to feed all his family. He was forced to go down the pit at the age of fourteen. What a tragic life he had led.

As I was saying, my main role models were males. If I wanted to be 'in' with them, then I had to join them in their way of life. I became pretty good at football. Mike's been quite surprised at my standard of play. Silly though it may seem, one of my most happy childhood memories was when I scored the winning goal in a game that I was playing with my three big brothers on the street. It was a header, and brilliant though I say it myself. The houses were all semi-detached, with a gate connecting the two separate blocks. There were no garages, no drives, just paths and a shared gateway. The gateway was the goal, so it was quite a small gap. My brothers were really impressed with me. I was the star of the match. They probably won't remember it, but it was very special to me. Very special.

So being "one of the boys" was easier and more natural for me than being a gentle female. That's not to say that I'm not gentle. I am. It's just that it's got to penetrate a lot of toughness to be seen. But God knows that. I know that God wants me to be a more gentle person. What type of daughter would I bring up if I didn't change my ways? Or son, for that matter. So I've put it to God. I've repented from not being the gentle person He wants. I've asked Him to bless me with the spirit of gentleness, one of the fruits of the Holy Spirit (Galatians 6:23). I continue to bind in the name of Jesus any spirit of the enemy which would try to prevent this happening. I daily ask the Holy Spirit to fill me, and do with me as He will. I try to remember to clothe myself with my "armour of God" (Ephesians 6:10-17). I always feel more able to cope with my lot once I've said what I believe God wants me to say. And I know that I am being changed. Praise God. There are certain things that I used to say and do that I wouldn't dream of repeating nowadays. I'm more sensitive to people who are hurting. He's changing me. I'm so thrilled, and grateful. And others must be very relieved.

To be fair to myself, one person did get down on her knees after hearing my story and gave herself to Jesus, but that was in July, 1990, *after* I'd come to accept that I was *not* a Billy Graham type evangelist.

July came. Early July. It was tea time, Sam was at a friend's house. The 'phone rang. "Hello, it's Joanne. How are you?" We had a chat about the family. Then it came. "I have another little girl to talk to you about, Dot. Shall I tell you a bit about her?"

"Please." And she did. I stood there listening. My heart was going bump, bump, bump and I felt this welling up of emotion inside me. "Joanne, can you tell me anything, well, *bad* about her?"

"No, Dot. I can't. There isn't anything." I could hardly believe my ears. And yet I could. She sounded, for want of a better word, perfect. I wanted to cry. "Talk to Mike about her, and then, if you'd like to go further, give me a ring in the morning and I'll get things moving." I looked at the clock. It was too late to 'phone Mike. He'd be home soon. Hurry up, Mike, I want to talk to you. As soon as he came through the door, I told him that Joanne had rung about another girl. I grabbed his hand and led him to the settee. "I want you to sit down next to me here on the settee and I'm going to tell you all about her."

So he sat down and I told him. Then I waited. "Well, you might as well go and fetch her now then," was his reply. "She's the one." Hurray!

The next day I could hardly wait to 'phone Joanne. She told me that she would contact the little girl's social worker and arrange for her, and probably her senior, to come and visit us.

And so it was that on the morning of Friday 14th July (Vive la France!) Mike and I were at home waiting (im)patiently for Joanne and two other social workers to come. On arrival Joanne introduced Marilyn, the little girl's own personal social worker and Anne, Marilyn's senior. They were two extremely nice, smart, kind, thoughtful ladies. Honest!

It was a bit strained to start with. It's a bizarre situation when you are meeting two people on whom you know you need to make a good impression, and yet not over do it. But, as we knew, we were going to be all right because it was all 'meant to be'. I made the drinks, then sat down on a dining chair, trying to appear calm and collected. Mike and Anne were on the settee, Joanne in one arm chair, Marilyn in another. I'm sure they must have marked me down as a nervous wreck!

Marilyn told us about the little girl. "Her name is Emma." My heart soared. She had a name. My daughter's name is Emma. Suddenly she took on a whole new meaning to me, now that I knew her name. Tears sprang to my eyes, "Emma," I whispered. I looked at Mike. He smiled. "Yes,

152

Emma Louise," said Marilyn, " and her birthday is 30th April and she's now 15 months old." Marilyn then went on to tell us more about Emma's background - about her Mum and Dad and about her foster parents, with whom Emma had been since birth. I listened, trying so very hard to concentrate, knowing, without doubt that she was the one. If I'd have been asked to write down the ideal background I'd have preferred for my future daughter, then this would have been it. It was almost too good to be true. Was this really happening? Marilyn finished telling us all about Emma. She waited for a reaction. I couldn't contain myself any longer and I burst into tears.

"She's the one. She's the one. She's just what we have been looking for in a daughter. I just can't believe it. Everything you've said to me is just what I've wanted in her background."

I had to go and get a tissue. Joanne asked me to sit next to Mike, who was sitting on the settee. Mike got all choked up. I couldn't speak. Mike continued for us. "It's hard to believe we've reached this stage after all we've gone through these past few years. I know that we've been led to believe that we *might* get a daughter at the end of the adoption procedure, but to actually reach this stage today, as we're all sitting here talking about Emma, it's wonderful, wonderful. It sounds as if she's just the little girl we've been wanting for so long. Well, it's quite hard to believe." And tears began to roll down his cheeks too.

The three social workers looked at each other. "It's lovely to see this reaction from them, isn't it?" Joanne said to Marilyn and Anne. No comment. Marilyn started to tell us what the procedure would be if we were accepted by them as adoptive parents for Emma.

I interrupted her emotionally. "I'm sorry," I blurted out, "but I can't see the point in you telling us what the procedure would be, unless you tell us that you'll allow us to apply for Emma." I felt tormented. "Can't you tell us now if you think we're all right for her?"

Marilyn and Anne looked at each other and Marilyn explained very kindly and patiently that she usually had to discuss things with Anne or another superior.

"Well, can't the two of you have a meeting here now?"

They looked at each other again. Anne said "We'll go out into the garden and have a chat." Off they went and I blew my nose and dabbed at my eyes. Mike blew his nose. Joanne smiled her lovely smile. They didn't take long. We all sat down again. Marilyn reached into her bag. "Would you like to see her photo?"

"Yes please," I said. When she asked me that question, I knew in my heart that this was it. That my dreams were all being realised. Marilyn gave me the photo and Mike and I both looked at it. What can you say? I must confess that I didn't automatically think " I love you" or " Aren't you beautiful?" It was more a " So this is the little girl I am going to love. She's the one who is the answer to all our prayers. She's the one God's had waiting for us." I felt so happy, so at peace. This photo was of our daughter. And she was so very, very precious.

Looking back, when I first saw Sam, I didn't automatically think " I love you, Sam," because, under the circumstances, I wasn't prepared for it. Indeed I was in shock. I didn't have that "bonding" which is so talked about in the text books and declared as so vital for a mother and baby relationship. But my love for Sam grew and I knew my love for Emma would grow.

Marilyn gave us more photos of Emma and of her Mum and Dad. They looked so nice, so good-looking. It was such a shame that Emma couldn't be with them, but then again, she was right for us and we knew that it was with God's blessing. Mike asked Marilyn what the procedure was to be. It began with another meeting, where the powers-that-be would formally agree to our approval for placement of Emma with us. That would probably be in about a week. It was, in fact, almost two weeks later, on Thursday 27th July, that we went to "panel" at 4.30 p.m. although we were not allowed to be present at the discussion, yet again.

It was our faith here again that helped us through this time. I can honestly say that I was never fraught. I kept reminding myself of Psalm 37:4, and Philippians, 4:5-7, and kept on saying my prayers. I felt great. Marilyn wanted us to meet Emma's foster mum before 27th July to plan a timetable for Emma's changeover. We chose Tuesday 25th, two days before. Mike asked that Emma not be there. He didn't want to meet her until the 27th, once all the papers had been signed. I could have seen her. I wanted to see her, but I knew God was teaching me patience. I remembered also that God had taught me through Ephesians 5:22 to obey my husband, especially on big issues, and this I knew was a big one. I certainly wasn't going to argue with him on anything concerning the adoption. I didn't want to and I knew God didn't want me to, and I knew I didn't need to. I was learning, slowly, and about time too!

I feel that I need to explain why and how I came to change my ways and accept that I should obey my husband. I first came across this Christian principle at a ladies fellowship meeting. We were looking at Ephesians 5:22-33. Verse 22 reads: "Wives, submit to your husbands as to the Lord." Well I'm sure that you can imagine what an extremely "lively" discussion we had about it. We quite liked what our husbands had to do. Verse 25; "Husbands, love your wives, just as Christ loved the church and gave himself up for her ,..." So our husbands had to be prepared to die for us. Quite right too if we had to obey them!

After the meeting I went home and mulled it over. Me, obey Mike, all the time. You must be joking! It's not that I ever deliberately disobeyed Mike or even wanted to. But to have a policy of always obeying him? Well it all seemed a bit too Dickensian to me. This was the 20th century after all. Surely God didn't want me to always obey Mike? I stood at the kitchen sink thinking it through. Surely God couldn't make me, force me to obey Mike. And then suddenly it dawned on me, and I laughed out loud. "Why God! You've already made me do it!" I laughed and laughed. He'd already made me obey Mike on an issue that I had refused to budge an inch on, namely the question of another baby. "Why You clever God!" I was so amazed at the way that God had gone about it all. I recalled how God had changed my stubborn attitude about adoption to 'obeying' Mike's wishes. I marvelled at the way in which God had worked it all out. Oh, God, You're so very, very clever! Well done!

After that episode I submitted to God's authority and accepted that I would always obey Mike on anything that was of any importance. And I can honestly say that God has really blessed our marriage through it. If any issue starts spoiling our relationship, I have found that by obeying Mike, and praying and asking God to sort out the problem (putting forward also my own personal solution to it all - yes, I am still human) then the matter will be resolved. I'm sure if he were asked, Mike would agree that I'm not a nagging wife. How fortunate I am, too, to have a husband who is open to being changed by the power of the Holy Spirit. I do so love it when God changes Mike's point of view to mine!

Tuesday the 25th arrived. It was yet another awkward situation. Can you imagine it, meeting Norma, the woman who has looked after your

155

child for the last 15 months? Mike and I had, of course said our prayers for this meeting. Indeed we had constantly been praying for every stage of Emma's adoption. I had now begun to ask lots of our Christian friends to pray for us, as we were so close to Emma coming to live with us.

And so we met Norma. What a truly wonderful woman. She had four adopted children of her own and had fostered many more. Emma was, in fact, her 27th foster child. Words fail me to describe her. She had so much love to give to children. You have to be a special type of person to be a foster parent. I certainly do not have Norma's qualities. I couldn't possibly have children from day one, knowing that, one day, someone is going to take them away from me and I might never see them again. I couldn't do it. It would break my heart. And yet Norma did it. And every time a child left her, she had a broken heart. Without fail. But her philosophy was that the children she cared for were deprived of their own, natural parents, so she, Norma, could *not* give them less than one hundred per cent of her love whilst they were under her roof. She couldn't give them ninety five per cent love, holding back some of herself so that she'd be protected when they left her. In her words " I love them whilst they're here, then have a broken heart for a few weeks when they've gone." She put the child's needs before hers. How marvellous. She always cared for two foster children at any one time, so that when one left she still had another to cuddle.

We didn't meet Doug, her husband, until the weekend. He too was an amazing man. Emma had, and still has, a great sense of humour and I'm sure that it was Doug who taught her to laugh. He was, to put a label on him, the clown. He'd do anything to make her laugh. And did she laugh. What a laugh she's got! Doug is special with a capital S.

We had provided Norma with an album full of photos of Mike, Sam and me, the house, each room in the house, the front garden and the back garden, so that Emma could be prepared for meeting us and moving into her new home. It had kept Emma entertained for quite a while.

When we met Norma, Marilyn gave us a suggested programme to move Emma over to us. It was so very well thought out. The idea was that, once we'd been approved, we'd immediately start the seven day plan.

Was it fate or divine power that Mike's firm had it's annual closure starting that week? Some might say "What a coincidence", but I prefer to use the Vicar's phrase and say "What a God - incidence!" God really is amazing! His timing is brilliant.

We received a 'phone call at 5.15 p.m. from Marilyn. "Yes, you've been accepted. Off you go and see her." Grandma had Sam. I rang Mike at work. He arranged to meet me at the end of Norma's road at a specific time. I arrived on time. Mike was late, held up by rush hour traffic. I sat in the car praying "Please Lord, bring Mike here quickly and safely. Please protect him. Fill me with peace, please, Lord. Let me greet him calmly." And I did. Praise the Lord. We tried to act calmly and tried not to appear too excited, walking hand in hand down the road. We wondered if the neighbours knew and were looking to see who was going to take Emma away from them. With hearts beating loudly we walked down the path. Just a few moments more and we'd be with our daughter. It was almost too much for my heart to bear.

Norma came to the door. We went into the house, into the hall. The lounge door was open. And there, toddling through it, was a little girl. I caught my breath. Was this her? Could it really be her? I knew it was because she was the little girl in the photo, but this was different. Here was a *real* girl.

"Hello," I said. "Hello." I didn't dare say her name. She looked up at me and, as our eyes met, she seemed to stop in her tracks and it looked as if she knew who we were. She had, of course, been well prepared by the photo album. And, as our eyes met there, a mini-miracle happened. We bonded. We both knew that she was my new daughter and I was her new mother. I walked over to her and knelt down. "Hello Emma. I'm your Mummy." I didn't touch her, I didn't dare and yet there was no need to. Then I saw Norma and I felt awkward for all of us. I felt that I was trespassing in some way. This was Norma's home and here I was, come to take her baby away. Norma went to make a drink. Mike and I sat on the settee. Emma toddled around. We sat there looking at her. She was so beautiful. And she was ours. It was like a dream. It was wonderful. I had an incredible sense of peace. I didn't need to rush anything. I had all the time in the world now. No need to rush Emma, or Norma.

We both felt a great deal of compassion for Norma. We held back initially from Emma purely out of consideration for Norma. We felt it only right to do so. We stayed for about an hour and went before it was too near

Emma's bed time. We wanted to have a good, happy first meeting with her before perhaps tiredness made her cry.

The next day, in the afternoon, Sam and I went to see Emma, for one hour. It went well. Norma had dug out some cars for Sam to play with, so he was happy. He'd been intrigued about meeting Emma, talking a bit about her on our drive to see her. Once there, he said "Hello," and enjoyed playing with all the toys with Emma and Kerry, Norma's other foster child. I suppose that his reaction was typical of a five year old boy meeting his new sister. When he'd met Lydia for the first time, he'd given her about ten seconds of his time, and then spent the rest of the time trying to work out how the incubator worked and why there were so many wires and tubes in his sister.

He was quite happy to kiss Emma goodbye and for me to kiss her. And then we came home. He didn't talk about her much. He talked more about the toys and Norma. He liked her. So far, so good. Praise the Lord. And then Mike finished work for the week and the seven day plan started. This was it.

Saturday 29th July:	Mike and Dot visit Emma.
Sunday 30th July:	Mike and Dot visit Emma. Stay for bed-time routine.
Monday 31st July:	Mike, Dot and Sam visit Emma. Go for an outing with Norma, Emma and Kerry.
Tuesday 1st August:	Mike, Dot and Sam visit Emma. Take Emma out without Norma.
Wednesday 2nd August:	Norma and Emma visit Ruddington. Transport by social worker.
Thursday 3rd August:	Mike or Dot collect Norma and Emma and go to Ruddington. Marilyn to collect Norma and take her home. Emma to stay for lunch. Emma to be returned to Norma's with Mike and Dot.
Friday 4th August:	Mike and Dot collect Emma. Stay for the day in Ruddington. Return for last night with Norma.
Saturday 5th August:	Mike and Dot collect Emma. Emma to stay for the night in Ruddington
Monday 7th August:	Return to Norma's for "Goodbye visit".

Marilyn had it all worked out very well. We were initially surprised that Emma would be moving in within only one week of us meeting her. But Marilyn explained that Emma mustn't get too used to us saying goodbye to her and leaving her at Norma's. It made sense.

The seven day plan worked perfectly. Thank you, Marilyn, thank You, God. Mike and I had never really prayed a lot together, but every morning, without fail, we'd start the day together in prayer, asking God to bless us all, Norma and her family included, and to help us through this time. We'd been told that it would be emotionally draining and that we would be whacked by the end of the week. Well, each evening we were tired, but it was more of a physical than an emotional tiredness. We were spending a lot of time travelling to and from Norma's house. It's a long way to Timbuktu and back again! We felt secure and confident about the whole thing. There were no negative feelings. Emma was absolutely fine with us. Sam was absolutely super with her. Mike and I felt absolutely at peace, seeing our two children together. Life was absolutely great. Praise the Lord!

There was only one negative about the whole episode, and that was the fact that Norma and her family were going to lose the child they loved. We were going to take their child away from them. It seemed so cruel. I know that Norma had gone through this 26 times previously and would volunteer to go through it again without batting an eyelid, but it did seem so very hurtful. What could we do to help them? Well, initially, we tried not to fuss over Emma too much in front of Norma, and then we realised that this wasn't being fair to Emma. I remember one instance when Emma fell over, smack bang in the middle of the two of us. We both started to go for her and then both held back to let the other 'mother' help. In the end I left Emma for Norma. What was at the back of my mind was "Emma will be totally mine soon. Let Norma enjoy her last few days with her." But I knew it was wrong. So after that I decided that I'd just have to take a more dominant role, for Emma's sake, and it felt right. Yet I knew that Norma was hurting inside. So Mike and I prayed. We knew that we could do nothing to help her ourselves, only God could touch her and give her His love and peace. Thank You, God.

There are two more points I'd like to mention about this changeover time. First, Once Emma had met Mike and I, she wouldn't settle at night in her cot. "She knows something's up," said Norma. She'd be crying and talking until really late at night before she'd finally go to sleep. Now we'd been told that, when she finally stayed with us, she would take some time to settle in. Well, as God is my witness, and indeed He is, that first night she slept at our home, she went to bed at her usual time of 8.00 p.m. and slept right through until 8.00 p.m. the following morning. She continued to sleep right through the night for a long time. This I know to be the result of God's hand on her. Each night when I went to bed, I would sneak into her room and pray over her. Then I'd sneak into Sam's room and pray over him. And, praise God, He answered my prayers. I still continue, nightly, to pray for them both. I must confess that there have been nights when it's simply been a quick "God bless Emma, God bless Sam", but I've known in my heart that they deserve and need more than that if they're going to survive in this rotten world. They need all the blessings which God has to offer.

Second point, on Monday 7th August Emma's official date of placement with us, we had to go back to Norma and Doug's house. Whilst there, Emma was supposed to say a final "goodbye" to all the rooms in the house and to Norma and to Doug. This was to assert that Mike and I were now looking after her and that Norma and Doug had no hold on her any more. Also it was to let Emma see that Norma and Doug were allowing her to go with us. As it turned out Emma cried shortly after we arrived. Then just before we left Norma got all upset and we had to dash out so that Emma didn't notice her crying. What a carry-on. We accepted that experts viewed this exercise as an important ingredient in the change-over process. We had been told of cases where children had never really settled into their new homes. It had been deduced that this was because the child had never actually had a clear signal from the foster-parents that they had said a final "goodbye". We all agreed later on that it had gone reasonably well, under the circumstances, but none of us had felt that it had been necessary. I wonder if God felt it had been necessary?

CHAPTER FIFTEEN

The Parties

Emma moved in with us officially on August 7th 1989. After a three month trial period there was a meeting at our house, to discuss how Emma had settled in. Joanne and Marilyn were there, and yet another social worker. We needed the latter's approval for our application to go in for Emma's formal adoption. Emma was a sheer delight during that meeting. The prayers of our Christian friends for the meeting had been answered. God was blessing us yet again. The social worker agreed that Emma looked very settled with us and agreed to our application. Praise God. Then, something happened to help me realise the type of "evangelism" God wanted me to do.

On Saturday 30th December 1989 I'd gone to bed thoroughly fed up with a phantom 'phone caller. We'd been having these calls for almost a week, and now the caller reckoned she wanted to meet me in the Victoria Centre, a huge shopping precinct in Nottingham city centre. I needed some advice. I'd asked God what He wanted me to do. I fell into bed and reached for my Bible. Would I perhaps find something from Him in here, I wondered?

He was to give me His answer through the Bible reading the next morning in church. The reading was Isaiah, 41:8-21. The caller had wanted to meet me. I'd do so if God wanted me to. This person obviously needed help even if she didn't realise it. And I knew God wanted to help her, because He loves her. However, the answer, in verse 12, was loud and clear; "though you look for them, they will not be found." I accepted that I'd be going on a wild goose chase.

I noticed a page of my Bible which was sticking out a bit at the bottom. Funny, I thought. I was usually so careful with it. I realised, on further examination, that it was a page that had been folded wrongly in its making and had been cut awkwardly, leaving a bit protruding. Why had I not noticed it before?

I looked at the page. It was in the book of Jeremiah, whoever he was. I'd not got around to reading all the Old Testament, even though I'd twice read the New Testament. The page included the end of chapter 29, all of chapter 30 and the start of chapter 31. I started to read chapter 30. "This is the word that came to Jeremiah from the Lord. This is what the Lord, the God of Israel says "Write in a book all the words I have spoken to you.""

I read no more. A revelation came to me. Recent happenings suddenly flashed before me and fused together to give me a vivid picture of what God wanted me to do. My sister-in-law in Canada had recently commented on how she enjoyed reading letters from me. They were nice and chatty. I acknowledged that I was a good letter writer. A friend from church had recently asked if she could ask me a personal question and my answer had been "Sure, my life's an open book!" And now shouting it out to me was this verse. He wants me to write a book! Could that be what He really wants me to do? Write a book? Of course, it was so obvious to me now. No problem! I felt quite excited. Why wasn't I feeling daunted at the task? God had prepared me well for this.

So that's what it was all about. Now I know that Jeremiah's words might not shout out to you as they did to me. I remember Graham, our vicar, once sharing with us at a Housegroup meeting how he'd been shown something by God and I hadn't grasped his interpretation of it. But it depends on the way the Holy Spirit explains what God's telling us, isn't it? It's different with everyone, because we're all different. Praise God.

I'd had this yearning to tell people, both Christians and non-Christians about what Jesus had done for me. That He'd helped me when I was at my wits end. That He'd taken away all my hurt and pain, that had become so unbearable. That He'd forgiven me for everything I'd done wrong. That He had stopped me from worrying about anything and everything. That He'd taken so many fears away from me. That I was now filled with joy and peace. That I had a beautiful little girl. That He was helping my son who had been unwittingly neglected throughout my years of grieving for lost babies and dead parents.

Oh, there was so much I wanted to tell them. That He wants them to stop worrying about anything. That He wants to take away any fears that they had about anything, other than a correct fear of Him. That He wants to help them and guide them every second of the day, not just to be turned to at times of crisis. That He is there with so much to give, if only He were asked. I would listen to people and their problems, and in my mind I'd be saying, Jesus can sort it out. He can solve that problem. He can take that fear away from you. He doesn't want you to worry about anything. Yet I seemed to lack the skill and the tact, needed to be able to express myself without being too forceful, too overpowering, too dogmatic. But here was my answer. Don't speak. Write! Oh, hallelujah!

So now I *could* do something about it. I could write a book. Brilliant. I was so glad. God had a job for me. What more could anyone wish for? To be told, specifically by God to do something. Please, I'm not decrying any of the many things that the Bible tells all of us to do every day. Not at all. Indeed, I have found it much easier at times to write this book than to accept the challenge of many verses of the Bible. I've been so happy doing it. I've felt so at peace, so content. Some people have been surprised how I've been able to find the time to write a book, what with having a young family. But as someone once said to me, "If God wants you to write a book, then He'll make the time available." And he was right. However, there have been times when I wanted to spend more time writing than I should have done. Because I wanted to get the book finished, so the whole world could read about what Jesus has done for me. However, the words never flowed so easily. I eventually realised that the family was being neglected and I wasn't getting any time to myself for relaxation. Although I was quite happy to forsake any time set aside for myself, God didn't want that. He didn't want me over-loaded. Satan did.

I thought it quite ironic that when I was at Grammar school, my teachers had readily entered me for all my "O" levels with the exception of my English Literature teacher, Mr Butterfield. I'd had to go and beg him to enter me for the exam. He'd done so but reluctantly. English Literature had always been such a bore to me - to read and analyse a book, to take it to pieces and to study each chapter in depth. Once I'd read a book I liked to leave it at that. I've never been one for reading the same book more than once. I think that the Bible's the only book that I've actually enjoyed reading more than once, well the New Testament at least. As stated above, I've still not read all the Old Testament. Shame on me. But now, here I was actually writing a book myself! It made me laugh! I've had no problem going over each chapter again and again, checking, correcting and analysing it. I've spent almost six years getting this book the way I believe God wants it. God's equipped me totally for this task. Nothing is impossible for God. Isn't He just wonderful?!

Writing a book was the form of "evangelism" which God wanted me to adopt, not *speaking* about what God had done for me. Oh, how I wish I'd realised all this sooner. Wisdom, wisdom. Patience, patience.

Application for adoption was duly made and we were given the date of 12th June 1990 at 10.40 a.m.. Mike's sister, Julia, and her family were to be visiting us during the month of July from Canada. So we thought that we could perhaps have a big "Christening Do" whilst they were here. We decided that we would combine Emma's christening with having our marriage blessed, or dedicated to use the correct terminology. It was something that had been on my mind for quite a time. I wanted some kind of formal ceremony in church to make more special what was already becoming a deeper and more loving bond between Mike and myself. Yes I knew that we had made a contract with each other in the Registry Office many years before, and that our relationship was now as solid as the Rock of Gibraltar. But I felt that it lacked something. It was the formal blessing of The Lord God Almighty. So we asked Graham to come round one evening to discuss the format and content of such a ceremony. That evening I learned something that I suppose in hindsight was extremely obvious. So often one can't see the wood for the trees!

I was explaining, very badly, why I wanted our marriage blessed. You see, when I'd married my first husband he was already divorced, so I didn't even consider a church wedding. I knew that it was out of the question. Yet I think that if we had been able to get married in church I wouldn't have been able to go through with it anyway. Whenever I'd been to church weddings I'd always felt somewhat in awe of the physical demands on the bride - being the centre of attention, with everyone's eyes on her, listening to her every word. Also the whole atmosphere of reverence within the church, those hushed conversations. The whole set-up was more than I would have felt able to cope with. But as it was, Allan was divorced so off to the Registry Office we had gone. Since I too was a divorcee when I had married Mike it was off to the Registry Office again, no other alternative considered. I was trying to explain to Graham and Mike why I felt awkward about church weddings. I was struggling to find the correct words.

"I couldn't have stood there in front of all those people and declared my vows to God. It would have been too much for me because....because...."

Graham finished my sentence for me. "Because you were a sinner. Yes, go on...."

I finished what I had to say and then the two men continued in conversation. I sat there and let the full impact of Graham's words sink in. Is that why I had always felt so uncomfortable about church weddings? Simply because I was a sinner? Surely it couldn't be as fundamental as that? But I could see now that it was. Thanks to the grace of God, I was no longer a sinner. Indeed I knew that I was now declared a saint in God's eyes. So I knew that I could stand before God and ask for His blessing on our marriage. What a revelation! It all seemed so obvious now that I knew. Talk about not seeing the wood for the trees. In front of me had been a mighty big forest!

About a week before going to court, we received a 'phone call from Emma's social worker, Marilyn. She explained that another social worker, whose job it was to fill in some more forms and visit Emma's natural mother to give her one last chance at changing her mind, was overloaded with work and could not possibly do the required visit and paperwork in time for June 12th. Marilyn would have to postpone the hearing. I was bitterly disappointed. Where had this other social worker sprung from? It was almost like a "whodunit" book, when the guilty one is only introduced in the last chapter. I felt cheated. We wouldn't be able to have the Christening in July after all. It was a blow. We prayed. We prayed for Emma's mum. It had been such a long, drawn out time for her. She needed God's help and God wanted to help her. He loved her.

A letter arrived. "Please note, the new hearing date for the above adoption is Tuesday 7th August 1990 at 10.20 a.m." I read the letter. August the 7th. I laughed. Oh, God, You are funny! How fitting that this date should be exactly one year, to the day, from Emma moving in. Her story began with a series of " God-incidences" and now it was ending with one. Some people would say that it was merely a coincidence that August 7th had been the date chosen by both the Social Services and the Crown Court, but I wouldn't. It was a "God-incidence". I felt very confident that this date was definite. We wouldn't have another postponement. I also felt quite encouraged when talking to Caroline, the lady who'd had the vision

165

about the little girl "daring" to open that box. Seven is a good Biblical number, she informed me. I didn't know that until she enlightened me. God made the earth in seven days, and seventy times seven I'm supposed to forgive my enemy. And our daughter was to become legally ours on the seventh. How about that!

So we went to court on that day and Emma was officially handed over to us. We'd prayed about it of course, asking God to bless this important milestone in Emma's life. So I was rather surprised when Sam suddenly announced in the car on our way to court that he was going to tell the judge that he didn't want a sister after all! Mike and I were both taken aback by this as I'm sure you can imagine. We hoped that Sam was merely joking. Some joke!

The judge hardly spoke to us. He seemed to direct all his questions to Sam. It could have been a disaster! "Are you going to look after her then? I know, you'll be horrible to her when you're a teenager. You'll tell her that you never wanted her, won't you?" he said with a wry, knowledgeable smile. I sat there in horror. I was extremely relieved to see Sam blush, and say all the "right" things. Praise God! We celebrated with toys for the children and a special lunch when we arrived home. Before we came home, we went to say thank you to God. Mike felt that he had to go to a Church. So we all went to St. Mary's in the Lace Market area of the city and said prayers of thanks for Emma and for Sam and for us. It was a church which Mike had attended occasionally at special services associated with his secondary school, the Nottingham High School. He had fond memories of it. Although it was my first time in that church I felt at peace in it. I could sense the presence of God there as we prayed.

Emma's birth certificate arrived. On it I was described by a new title. For mother's profession, it said "homemaker". It was the new Social Services word to replace "housewife". I do so like that word. "I'm a homemaker." Sounds so much more dignified than housewife! So, ladies, remember - homemaker!

The Christening and Marriage Dedication could now at last take place. We decided to leave it until after Christmas.

I now need to return to a subject which I mentioned much earlier in the book, the subject of speaking in tongues. It was 6th November, 1990. Graham, our regular weekly House Group "leader" was talking about "speaking in tongues". I listened intently to his teaching. I took it all on

166

board. Yes, I knew that speaking in tongues was one of the gifts that God gave to reborn Christians. But somehow I just didn't seem able to do it. He had blessed me with so much already. Perhaps He didn't want me to have this one. Was I being too greedy?

Graham's teaching that night was a revelation to me. He explained that speaking in tongues was one of the *least* of the gifts given by God. I had somehow thought that it was a special gift only given to "special" people. Yet I knew that in God's eyes we are all special! Having read 1 Corinthians 12:1-11, in which all the gifts are listed, and after counselling, I'd come to accept that God had chosen to bless me at that time with the spiritual gift of faith. I'd supposed, wrongly, that this particular gift of tongues was not one with which God wished to bless me. In hindsight, one of Satan's minions had been having a heyday with me.

Tonight Graham was expounding on the subject and showing us through scriptures that the gift was indeed for all, if they wanted it. Well I didn't know about the rest of the housegroup, but I knew darned well that I wanted it. I told the group that I'd wanted to speak in tongues for *ages*. I'd read some books when I first became a Christian and had been bowled over by the sheer power of Christians being used by God to voice His prayers on earth. "Chasing the Dragon" - the story of a young missionary woman, Jackie Pullinger, being used by God to help the drug addicts in China, spoke so dramatically of the power of the Tongue. If God wanted to use me, then I was raring to go. But I just could not manage it. The housegroup prayed for me. Graham laid hands on me, along with Mike who'd recently started praying in tongues - adding much to my frustration, as I'm sure you can imagine!

I opened my mouth, hoping to be taken over by the Holy Spirit and to burst forth in beautiful sounds, just like those described in the books I'd read. Nothing happened. Oooo, I felt *so* frustrated. What was I doing wrong? I'd heard other people praying in tongues. One lady from my church had come round to see me one evening to talk about the gift of tongues which she'd eventually discovered whilst relaxing in the bath. I'd tried that. I'd tried putting a Christian music tape on full blast whilst doing the vacuuming in an attempt to "relax". That had been Gill's suggestion. It was no good. I couldn't do it. Failure. Again.

I convinced myself that because I was a language teacher, God didn't want me to have another language. But no. I knew He did. I turned to the

Bible, Acts 2, and read the account of the Holy Spirit arriving at Pentecost. And there I read verse 4 again and again. "All of them were filled with the Holy Spirit and began to speak in other *tongues* as the Spirit enabled them." (A footnote gave the alternative translation "or *languages*") It didn't say that *some* of them began to speak in other tongues, but that *all* did.

I decided I'd had enough. This was going to be sorted out once and for all. That Sunday I would go to the Congregational Church in the city centre. It was where a former teaching colleague of mine worshipped. Alice had been an R.E. teacher at Fairham Comprehensive when I was teaching there and we'd recently made contact again.

She'd come round to see me, and told me about her church. Apparently there were no formalities there, no set format to the services at all. People worshipped, shared their testimonies, danced in the aisle and prayed in tongues. They seemed to have no inhibitions. This, I decided, was just what I needed. I'd told Alice that I didn't pray in tongues and that I desperately wanted to. Alice had said she'd pray for me. She reckoned that we'd both had the same stumbling block. But she'd got over hers. Now it was my turn.

Having told her I was going, Alice was waiting for me outside the church. It was so thoughtful of her. I still become overwhelmed when people do "nice" things for me. It seems to touch a raw nerve somewhere. To think, when we were both teaching colleagues we had never had any intimate conversations. Now, well, we knew that we were sisters, and behaved as such. How civilised! We embraced and went in. I didn't feel nervous, indeed I was extremely excited. I just knew that something was going to happen here tonight. I could feel it in the air. I told Alice so. She told me she'd been praying for my speaking in tongues. I told her that tonight was the night.

"What's the format as regards praying in tongues? Do you pray in tongues every Sunday? Who starts it off? Is it the preacher?"

Alice just smiled. "Don't worry, Dot. It'll happen."

Me - worry? Never!

It was November 11th. Armistice Day. I asked her if their morning service had been like ours - completely dedicated to the event.

"Oh no. We had two minutes silence, and then we carried on as usual." How different this church was to my own. The service began. We praised Jesus. I felt very emotional. I told Alice that I'd probably cry. She said that people often did. She might! We sang two or three praiseworthy choruses, and then there was a pause.

Alice began singing in tongues. Somebody else did, then another. It seemed as if everyone was singing in an incomprehensible language. I couldn't make out what they were singing about. Was the language teacher in me *still* trying to translate the words? I shrugged my shoulders. If you can't beat 'em, join 'em. So I did. To start with I'm sure I copied one or two of the sounds that Alice was emitting. Then I gave up, or surrendered, or Satan lost his grip on me, call it whatever you will. And I began singing in tongues.

I have to confess that it was not as earth-moving an experience as I had thought it would be. I had not felt "taken over" by another voice as I had imagined I would. I was still totally in control. A word or sound was there on my lips, just as words are springing from my mouth as I now put pen to paper, but there was none of the 'possession' that I had been afraid of. I'd thought that the Holy Spirit would completely take control of my voice box. How Satan had tricked me. I was actually saying *voluntarily* the sounds and words which the Holy Spirit was bringing to my mind.

I stood there, tears streaming down my face, down Alice's too, and I was so very, very happy. I was singing in tongues. Hallelujah! I can't remember what the sermon was about - sorry! But there was more in store for me that night. Alice told me that Jesus had brought to her mind Numbers 11:17. She turned to it and read it to me : "I will come down and speak with you there, and I will take of the Spirit that is on you and put the Spirit on them...". She felt that He wanted her to bless me with the spiritual gifts with which she indeed had been blessed. So she prayed for me. I felt so overwhelmed at this, more so than I had been with finally speaking in tongues. I'd come asking for one blessing and had been offered more.

This has happened to me so many times. I've asked for help in one area, received it and been given even more. His generosity is never-ending. I become so choked up when I think of His goodness to me. I know that I don't deserve His goodness, not at all. Yet He still continues to pour blessings onto me. I went home full of joy. I walked along the road singing in tongues, then drove all the way home singing. I was amazed that I didn't have to concentrate on it at all. If I'd been singing a song in

English, or in French, I would subconsciously have been thinking "what comes next?". Not so with this language. Because it was totally unknown to me. I had to laugh at myself. I'd been looking at it far too intellectually as a lot of people had suggested might be my problem.

Later I realised that I had in fact sung in tongues before, but had not realised it. It had been whilst I'd been vacuuming. I was singing a Christian song. I'd forgotten the words half-way through and had started, so I thought, to make up some words to fill in the gaps. But they hadn't been the usual la la la or tum ti tum, but to my mind silly non-sensical utterings.

I arrived home. Mike looked up at me. I gave him a huge smile. "I speak in tongues!" Mike was so very pleased for me, and for him! I don't think I could have coped with him speaking fluently in tongues whilst I couldn't. I might have made the going tough for him. There was still a lot of the old me yet to be sorted out, and there still is!

I had to go back to that church about a month later for reassurance that I was speaking in tongues and not uttering a load of gibberish. One of Satan's minions, was having a go at me. He was saying that I could not possibly be speaking in tongues because, in the books which I had read, the Spirit-filled Christians all spoke of a beautiful language bursting forth. And I didn't have this feeling. The language which I was speaking was quite hard and harsh-sounding. I'm a French teacher and love the romantic sounds of this Latin-based language. I'd not been turned on the same way by German. It had been too harsh-sounding for me, and I was always one to cringe at a broad American accent.

And now I was uttering harsh-sounding words myself. It seemed most peculiar, unnatural. But, of course it wasn't natural. It was supernatural. When it came to a time for individual ministry at the Congregational church, I went forward and explained what I thought was happening to me. A man prayed for me, after confirming that this was a typical ploy of the enemy to try and stop me from doing what the Lord wanted me to do. As he prayed I felt a tremendous presence going through me. I felt wonderful. I felt as if I could have floated. I'd watched this man ministering to others as I had waited in a queue. He'd prayed for a lady who had swooned in front of him and had been helped to lie down by 'helpers'. A man had followed her. He was prayed over and he, too, swooned and was helped to lie down. I watched all this, eyes agog. I'm not going to him for ministry, I thought! I'd intended to go to one of the people I knew to be church elders. This man was unknown to me. By sight he looked so ordinary, in his dark blue suit and glasses. No, I wanted to go to an elder, someone of status. Oh you vain creature. It's the same Holy Spirit working through him as is in the elders of the church. What difference does it make who ministers to whom? God will equip his soldiers with the necessary kit for fighting.

His prayer? It was very simple and to the point. He kept on shouting the name of Jesus over me time and time again. It's effect had been enough to make me start to swoon as well. I can't do this, I thought, and really fought to stay upright. Looking back I wish I hadn't. I wished I'd given in to the wonderful feeling I'd had and basked in the presence of Jesus' love and power. As it was, I went home totally assured that I was speaking in tongues. Praise God.

It was Christmas 1990. One of my presents from Mike was a paperback, "How to get a Book Published." He thought it might help me. It informed me that I was going about this book in totally the wrong way! Help! Apparently, once you've decided to write a book, you should first approach publishers until you find one who is prepared to consider the completed work. Then, you don't waste your time writing a book which no publisher wants.

Oh well, I thought, I've got it all wrong again, haven't I? And then I thought, well, no, I'm sure I haven't. If God's told me to write a book, then I don't need to go hunting for a publisher so early. I'll write it, then present it to a publisher. It'll get published. The proof is in the reading!

It seemed like an answer to prayer when I bumped into Caroline. I was having a cup of coffee in the Lantern, the Christian cafe in the village. I found myself sitting next to one of the ladies who had helped to set it up "What are you doing now?" she asked.

"I'm writing a book."

"Really? What sort of book?"

"A Christian book. It's my testimony."

"Do you have a publisher?"

"No, I haven't got that far. But God's told me to write a book, so I'll find one."

"Well, perhaps I can help you there."

"How?"

"Well, I'm now working in the publishing department of the Assemblies of God in Talbot Street, Nottingham. If you like, I'll write you a list of the chief Christian paperback publishers." I could hardly believe my ears. And yet I could. This was amazing. A gift from God. I felt any pressure to go hunting for a publisher just disappear. God is so good! I did apply to several of these publishers, only to be turned down by them. What a blow to my pride that was. I realise now that God wanted to deal with several issues with me before the book would finally go to print.

I did not however end up using any of these Christian publishers. My husband, Mike, felt a nudge to have a go at publishing it. My good friend, Karen, a brilliant artist in my opinion, was delighted to design a cover for me. The Lord provides....

The Lord then gave me another gift. Although I can go plink-plonk on a typewriter and type a letter to someone, I chose to write my book long-hand because it flowed so readily from my pen. So I needed a typist. Mike reckoned that I needed someone who could type it onto a computer disk, then he could transfer it onto his computer and print it using his printer. It all seemed fairly straight forward. That is, of course to someone who knows nothing about computers. I didn't appreciate, at that time, that different computers use different types and sizes of disks. All the agencies I tried used different sized disks from ours. What had seemed a simple problem was becoming increasingly difficult. Surely if God knew that I'd written this all long-hand, He knew that I needed someone with a computer compatible with ours. Where was that person? I'd prayed about it all, but I was getting absolutely nowhere by going to the agencies. I felt like giving up. Then it happened. Wonderfully. Effortlessly. The way it usually is with God.

One afternoon I was having a cup of coffee with a Christian acquaintance, Cathy. She has a daughter the same age as Emma. We had agreed to meet for an hour one afternoon. Our children were happily playing in Cathy's lounge. I was exasperatedly telling Cathy about all my problems as regards finding a typist.

"If you're struggling I could always have a go at typing it for you," she said, nonchalantly. She pointed to a computer next to which Emma and Naomi were playing.

"Pardon?" I asked. "Do you type?"

"Yes, most of the work I do is typing."

Talk about being flabbergasted. Guess what? The disks used were the same size and the software was compatible. Hallelujah!

It's been wonderful having Cathy to help me with the book. She's been able to give me such valuable advice. And she's supported me when at times I've felt ready to pack it all in. I've certainly been 'got at' at times throughout the writing of this book. At one point I was going to throw it all in the bin, convinced that the enemy had inspired the writing of this book. They knew that my Achilles' heal was rejection. If my non-Christian family and friends were to read the book then they'd not want to talk to me again, the enemy were telling me. The book would upset them. But, praise God, it's finished. My family have read a rough draft to agree that everything is as accurate as possible. And we're all still talking!

Our Christening and Marriage Dedication Service took place on Sunday February 3rd. Mike and I had to consider again the question of Godparents. We had not wanted anyone but ourselves to be Sam's Godparents. We'd felt that we alone should be in charge of his Christian upbringing. This time, though, we felt completely different about the event, and asked the whole congregation to be Emma's Godparents! I found it quite touching after the service when one of the congregation said he might pop round some time to see his God-daughter! We felt at peace welcoming Emma into God's family. We knew what we were undertaking - to bring her up according to God's ways, with submission in her heart to Jesus, the Man who had given His life for her. How we had been changed since Sam's Christening! It was a truly blessed day. Blessed in so many differing ways. We'd obviously been asking God to bless the whole event and indeed He did. We asked Him for a miracle and He gave us one. He was so good, so gracious to us that day, it was wonderful.

Emma, at the age of 2 years and 10 months, did not protest at being baptised. A friend had told me how her three year old daughter had done so at her Christening. I asked God to sort Emma out on that one. He did. Thank You, God.

As I knelt at the front of the church with Mike, and Graham asked God to bless our marriage, I felt so very, very content there. I was amazed that I wasn't nervous and could thoroughly enjoy the whole event. And my relationship with Mike is getting better all the time, maturing like a good port wine!. Praise God.

The weather was not too inclement to stop people travelling from as far north as Manchester and as far south as London. For February that was pretty good going.

As for the miracle. Well, a friend of mine, who knew the full gospel, was in the congregation. She had been "umming and ahhing" about whether to respond to God's invitation to salvation for some time. That day she chose to become a Christian. So there was a party going on in Heaven as well as on earth!

CHAPTER SIXTEEN

The Anniversary

It was March 1990. Life was reasonably fine. The children were fit and healthy. So were Mike and I. Mike was getting a lot of hassle at work but he was tackling it with prayer, and feeling that he was coping fairly well. Emma's second birthday was approaching. I'd decided that we were going to have a big family "do". Her second but our first.

I started to talk to Emma about her birthday as mothers do. "Shall we have a party then? Lots of cakes and jellies. How many candles shall we have? - two?" But Emma wasn't too fussed about it. She made an awful noise that could be likened to the mewing of a dying cat! Then pouted and shouted "No" at me. Wonderful aren't they at that age? Praise God for children!

She became ill. A virus or something similar. And she was sick. She kept on being sick, every day without fail at about tea-time. I tried starving her for twenty-four hours and then giving her dry toast and arrowroot biscuits. You name it and I was giving it to her, including lots of prayer. "Please, Jesus, put Your hand on Emma and heal her."

But she wasn't getting any better. She was getting worse. I couldn't understand it. Why wasn't she getting better? Whenever I'd asked for healing before, we'd been given it. Why not now? And it was Emma who was suffering. "Please, Jesus, please heal Emma."

I'd taken her to the doctor, who said that it was a virus. There was nothing that he could give to cure her. Nature would just have to take her course and Emma would get better eventually. Nothing anybody could do. Well I'm sorry but I couldn't agree with that. Not now I was a Christian. There was something I could do. Pray. So I did. And I asked other Christians to pray for her. Meanwhile, after three weeks of being sick virtually every day, Emma was losing a lot of weight, and her complexion

175

became grey. She had no energy to do anything. She was as weak as a kitten. She wanted and needed me to carry her everywhere, cuddle her at all times, and cried whenever I put her down. I kept trying to cheer her up and tried to be positive. I'd try and play games with her, but she wasn't interested in anything.

After three weeks, one Friday morning, I went back to the doctor. Surely there was something he could do? He suggested that I might try penicillin. It might help, but he doubted it very much. I took the prescription home but never actually fetched the medicine. I felt wrong giving her penicillin when in my heart I knew that it couldn't get rid of the virus. But I knew that Jesus could. Why, then, wasn't He healing her? Had I done something wrong? Had I offended Him? Had He stopped healing us? I was starting to think in a most negative way. I knew that I was getting it all wrong again. Stop it, Dorothy, you know God doesn't work like that. The Accuser was at work again. Get behind me, Satan. I kept on praying for Emma. What else could I do?

The morning I'd seen the doctor and been given the prescription, I was walking back home and passed Gill, who was in her car. She pulled up and asked after Emma's health. I've found it so invaluable having so many Christians living nearby, enabling me to have a chat to when I've needed it. And God knew my need that day, and was going to use Gill to help me. Praise God. I told her what had happened in the doctor's, and then couldn't hold back the tears any more. "She's not getting better, Gill. And I keep on asking Jesus to heal her and He hasn't. I'm worn out. I just don't understand. He always answered my prayers before, Gill. Why won't He heal her? She's my daughter. It's awful when she's just lying there groaning and being sick. I can't take much more of this. And it's her birthday this weekend. She was going to have a big party. I've had to cancel it."

Gill's face lit up. "Is it Emma's birthday?" she asked. "I was telling Graham that Emma wasn't getting better, and he asked me when her birthday was. I thought it wasn't for another couple of months."

"No, it's on Monday."

She smiled at me. "I'll come and see you this afternoon, Dot."

I walked back feeling glad I'd had a good cry about it. There's a limit to what I could take. It had all been so draining for me to see my beautiful Emma suffering so. I was emotionally and spiritually whacked.

Gill didn't come and see me that afternoon. Graham did. "How is she, Dot?" he was genuinely concerned. He really is a most caring and loving shepherd of his flock.

"Look at her, Graham. She's grey. I just don't understand it. I keep on praying for healing and nothing's happened. It doesn't make sense."

He smiled one of his smiles that meant he was going to help sort me out yet again. He explained to me that sometimes when someone needs healing they might need a different prayer from the one being said. Sometimes it needed to be a more precise prayer. The actual cause of the illness might need to be prayed about. He then went on to tell me that sometimes God can speak into a situation with what is known biblically as a "word of knowledge". This can actually pin-point the root of the problem. When Gill had first spoken to Graham about Emma, the word "anniversary" had sprung into his mind. He'd asked Gill if Emma had some anniversary coming up, and Gill had said that she thought not. Until I'd bumped into her that morning. So that's why he'd come round.

He asked me if I was still with him in understanding what he was talking about. Yes, I could understand him so far. He continued.

It says in the Bible that when Jesus was alive He healed the sick and cast out evil spirits and demons.

"Could I accept that," he asked?

Yes, yes. I didn't understand much about spirits and demons, but I accepted what the Bible said. If it said Jesus did it, then He did.

"Now then," (Graham uses that phrase quite a lot) "there's the Holy Spirit. And there are other spirits. Good and bad. They're in the heavenly realm. Just like bugs. We get earthly bugs, like colds, 'flu and so on, and there are also spiritual bugs. But there's no need to be afraid of them, because at the name of Jesus they *have* to go." He said that quite emphatically.

"Was I still with him?" he asked.

"Sort of."

"Well Emma has a bug. A spiritual one. A spirit of anniversary. It probably sneaked in her at birth. And it needs to go."

I thought hard. Well it sort of made sense. It must have been an awful experience for her and her Mum at the birth. Emma had spent nine months inside a woman who had rejected her at conception, had decided to give her up for adoption. How traumatic it must have been for Emma's

177

Mum to have gone through all the hormone changes that occur during pregnancy, and through all the physical pain of childbirth, knowing that it was all to be for nothing. What emotional turmoil all round. What could have happened to Emma when she was being born, from the womb of a woman who was going to give her away? I would like to add here that I know that Emma's Mum came to love her baby - what woman couldn't? She has a birth photo of Emma which she told me she kissed every night, and tells Emma that she loves her.

A spirit of anniversary. Was it that which was making Emma so ill? Then I remembered that my Mum had died on New Year's Day 1957, and I always felt depressed on that date every year. It seemed doubly hurtful to me, because that day was for everyone else a time of rejoicing. I used to try and enjoy New Year's Eve parties but usually knew that I couldn't be truly myself. Conversely, when I did have a good time, I'd feel guilty about it a day or two later. How dare I enjoy myself at such a time? Did I have a spirit of anniversary?

Graham said he'd like to pray over Emma if he may. I certainly had no objections. I welcome all prayers at any time for me and my family. Emma was sitting on my knee. Graham placed his hands on her head and began praying. He prayed in his native tongue and then in the tongue of the Holy Spirit. I was tremendously moved by Graham's prayer. I felt a tremendous feeling of peace. Tears were streaming down my face. I was so relieved that these weeks of agony were almost over, that Jesus was healing her. He ended his prayer, claiming in the name of Jesus that, from that day on, birthdays would be truly happy occasions for Emma. When he'd finished, I took her off my knee and stood her up. She stayed there. She didn't cling to me. She didn't cry. She actually stood there. By herself.

She was healed. I knew it. Thank you, Jesus. Thank you, Graham. She held my hand and we walked with Graham to the front door to show him out.

"Thanks, Graham."

"That's all right. Any time. But it's not me who healed her you know." He went away with a smile on his face. Yes, Graham, I know. It was Jesus. I apologised to Jesus for saying that He wasn't healing her. He had done. But I'd been saying the wrong prayer. I'd been asking for physical healing when it was spiritual, emotional healing which she had

178

needed. Thank God for Graham. 'Words of knowledge'. 'Spirits'. It had all been new to me. But Emma was better. That was all that mattered.

Shortly after Graham left, Emma went outside to play with her new football. I couldn't believe the transformation in her. And yet I could. I still kept the party cancelled, because she was still convalescing. Although she was now spiritually healed, her body was still weak from the constant sickness. She needed to take it steady for her body to recover. It took about two weeks to build her back to her former state of health.

But spiritually she was fine. Absolutely one hundred per cent. For a start I couldn't stop her singing "Happy birthday to you". It could have driven us all spare! Before Graham's arrival the mere mention of the word 'birthday' had made her react unfavourably. If we'd tried to sing 'Happy Birthday', she'd have been very upset. But the illness had gone. Jesus had taken it away. Wonderful. Fantastic. And having taken on board Graham's teaching, I asked Jesus to heal me spiritually in the same way. Now I no longer get depressed around New Year's Day. Praise the Lord!

I know that some people have found it hard to accept that I have discovered a peace in Christ, after losing my first daughter. How can I acknowledge the existence of a loving God when so much tragedy has befallen me, they ask. Surely a loving God wouldn't allow Lydia to have been born Down's Syndrome? Well, I do believe I have discovered the answer.

In my Bible readings, I came across the book of Job. I didn't know anything about him. I'd often heard, and indeed used the phrase - "To have the patience of Job." But I had no idea who he was, or what his story was. When I read the story, I found it absolutely fascinating, frightening and revealing. For those people who have not studied the book of Job, 1:1 sums him up very well: "In the land of Uz there lived a man whose name was Job. This man was blameless and upright; he feared God and shunned evil." In an extremely small nutshell, the story is as follows: God allowed the devil to test Job's faith by causing the death of his animals, his servants, his seven sons and his three daughters. He also inflicted Job "with painful sores from the soles of his feet to the top of his head." (2:7.) There's a lot more to the story than this, but that's all I need to mention for my own purposes.

I marvelled that Job could cope with his lot. Could I have survived such a string of disasters? One particular verse in the book (3:25) spoke directly to me. In it, Job says; "What I feared has come upon me; what I dreaded has happened to me." I let that verse sink in. So, although Job knew God and feared Him, he was still afraid of other things. He must have feared the loss of all his animals. He must have feared the loss of all his servants. He must have feared losing his sons and his daughters. He must have feared his painful sores. And, because he had fearfully anticipated those events, they had happened. The devil had found a foothold. Yet he knew, in his heart, that he should fear only the wrath of God.

My fear had been the possibility of having a socially unacceptable, mentally handicapped daughter. And that's what I did have, i.e., what I had perceived at that time as a socially unacceptable mentally handicapped daughter. I'd feared it. So I'd got it. My mind was in a whirl. So, if I'd not been scared of having a Down's Syndrome baby I'd not have had one.

But I hadn't intentionally feared having a mentally handicapped daughter. I don't really know where that fear had come from. But I knew that it was there. I wasn't trying to deny that I had this inner fear. I acknowledged that I had hardly come across any Down's Syndrome children, I could count the number of them on one hand. That was most probably my problem. Plain, simple ignorance.

When I prayed about this fear and wondered where it had come from, I was reminded of an occasion when I'd been stopped as I was walking to work by a Down's Syndrome child. She was about thirteen or fourteen years of age, the age group which I was used to teaching. She was walking with a lady who was most probably her Mum. The girl suddenly grabbed hold of my arm and started talking to me. She wanted to know my name. I felt overcome with embarrassment. I didn't know how to talk to her. I'd never spoken to a mentally handicapped person before. I lied. I told her an imaginary name. The teacher I was walking with looked at me in amazement. When asked, Sue told the young girl her true name. The Mum prised the girl away from me and carried on her way. I walked on with my colleague. We didn't mention what had just happened. Why on earth had I lied? It didn't make sense. I had not deliberately shunned the presence of these people. Perhaps I had unwittingly tried to avoid them because of an inner fear, and had just not realised it. I only knew that I had an inner fear of them, which was obviously not what God wanted.

I started listening to people with tragedy in their lives. I would, as casually as possible, ask them if their situation had been something they'd dreaded, consciously or sub-consciously, and it was. Now I'm not saying that every tragedy is a result of someone or other's fear. Not at all. I'm saying that I believe that God was putting these people in front of me on purpose. He wanted to get across to me that I was on the right track. It was all to do with fear. It all seemed to fit. I pondered some more.

I concluded that if I'm to be the way God wants me to be, then I'm to fear nothing and no one - only God, who loves me. Who loves me enough to allow His innocent Son to die an awful, shameful death for me.

So I put it to God. "If there are things, or people that I'm scared of, I'm sorry. I repent. Please show me who, or what they are and help me to stop being scared of them." I was amazed and horrified at what and who scared me. God has shown me areas of my life where there have been many fears. I could write a book purely on the fears which have stopped me from enjoying so much that which God would wish me to enjoy. In fact I do believe that that is what the Lord wants me to do next.

CHAPTER SEVENTEEN

Epilogue

Up until 1986, if anyone had asked me, "Was I a Christian?" I'd have instinctively said that I was. I'd been christened. I believed in the story of Jesus. I believed that He was born in Bethlehem roughly two thousand years ago. I believed He performed miracles - healing the sick, changing water into wine, bringing the dead back to life. I believed that He was crucified. I believed He was seen three days later by hundreds of people. I believed He had gone up into Heaven. I believed that He was the Son of God. I'd never had any reason to doubt any of these things. I believed it all. I'd accepted what the reputable history books said. Why shouldn't I? I believed He was my friend. I remember singing "What a friend we have in Jesus" whilst at Sunday School. He was my friend, and I believed I'd be with Him one day, when I went to Heaven, because that's where He was, with my Mum. So often as a child I'd wanted to die and go and be in Heaven with Jesus and my Mum. I'd be happy there. Heaven sounded a lovely place.

One of the few Bible quotations which I knew by heart was John, 3:16, the verse which is acclaimed to be the most famous one in the Bible. It's the one that is quoted in the front of the famous Gideon Bibles which are found in hospitals and hotels. "For God so loved the world that He gave his one and only Son, that whoever believes in him shall not perish but have eternal life." I believed. So I believed that I would not perish and that I would have eternal life.

But I had not known the true meaning of the word "believe" in this verse. I didn't know that it meant I had to put Jesus in charge of my life, of my present plans and my eternal destiny. One of Satan's minions had really done, a good job deceiving me. He led me to believe that I was a

182

Christian. But I wasn't. I wasn't a Christ-i(a)n. Christ wasn't *in* me. My belief was merely superficial.

I was so wrong. I only knew part of the story of Jesus. What is it they say? "A little knowledge can be dangerous?" It was almost fatal for me. And indeed, when I think of all the things I've done wrong, what an insult it was to Jesus, to call myself a Christian, a follower of Christ. It all could have been avoided if only I'd known then what I know now. If only.....

But hasn't God been good in showing me where I was going wrong? Hasn't God been so merciful towards me? Hasn't He been so generous and kind and loving and forgiving to me? Isn't He marvellous? He's never told me off for having misunderstood the gospel for so long, for having been so ignorant of so much of His word, for not studying John 3:16 in its full context. He's never condemned me, as I and the enemy have done. He's welcomed me with open arms, just as He did with the prodigal son. And isn't Jesus wonderful, the way He's helped me to have such a fabulous relationship with God the Father, through dying for me? For me!

I know that I don't deserve any of the blessings which have been showered upon me since Jesus found me. I have committed some horrendous sins. But I've been forgiven. I no longer shudder when I think of those times when I sinned. Praise God. He's freed me from those feelings of guilt. And all I've done is say that prayer of repentance, and claimed Jesus as my Lord. The effect has been life-saving. Under the guidance of God and Jesus and the Holy Spirit, my eyes have been opened to the sheer magnitude of their power. And their love for me.

As for my daughter, Lydia, it is no longer of such dire importance to know her *exact* whereabouts. I have my own *opinion* about that, though some theologians might take me to task about it. But nobody can upset me about the subject any more, because I know that Jesus is alive and looking after her for me, and that, one day, I'll see her again. I know because I'm a born-again Christian, because I have eternal life and because Jesus tells me so in John 3:3.

I do not now know if I will find my mother when I am called to Heaven. One evening I went to see a lady from the Pentecostal Bethel I used to go to as a child. I'd discovered that we had donated our enormous family Bible to the Bethel, and I was enquiring as to it's whereabouts. The lady who had run the Bethel when I was there popped in to say "Hello" to me. She knew my Mum. I dared myself to ask her a question which had been on my heart for a long time. "Did my Mum know the Lord?"

She smiled at me very kindly. "No, dear. She didn't." My worst fears had been realised. "Then again, dear, she might have done at the end. You never know. You'll find out one day."

I'd been so devastated to find this out. But I'd had my fears about it for some time. I'd asked myself many times if my Mum had been a believer or a reborn Christian. I shed many, many tears that week for my Mum. Then I asked God to have mercy on her soul, and carried on with my life. What else could I do?

I now thank the two Jehovah's Witnesses for upsetting me that day, years ago. Was it one of Satan's minions who sent them to upset me or was it God Himself? God knew that He would be able to bring good out of it. He knew that as a result of them upsetting me, I'd come to know Jesus. If it was not for them insisting that my daughter was not in Heaven and making me ask myself "Where is Lydia?" I might never have discovered what I needed to. I might never have been able to walk around with my head held high, living in the knowledge that I have nothing, absolutely nothing, to fear from this horrible, evil world. I have the Creator of the universe as my personal helper, comforter and guide, and I am so amazingly, wonderfully, mind-blowingly loved. Did I deserve such goodness, such kindness from Him? No, I deserved nothing. Yet He has given me so much. What a wonderful Father I have.

APPENDIX 1

These are the Bible references from my confirmation course, with thanks to Graham Harrison:

Session one

Genesis, 1:1 - 2:4
Hebrews, 11:3
Psalm 19:1
Romans, 1:20
Hebrews, 1:1-2
Colossians, 1:15

Session two

Genesis, 1:26-28;
Genesis, 2:15
Ephesians, 1:4-5
Genesis, 3:8-9
John, 14:23

Session three

Isaiah, 64:6
Romans, 3:20
Galatians, 2:15-16
Luke, 9:20
Ephesians, 1:9-10

Matthew, 16:16
Mark, 14:61
Luke, 3:22
Luke, 9:35
John, 1:1-3 and 1:14
John, 6:38
John, 8:58
Philippians, 2:5-11
Colossians, 1:15-18
Hebrews, 1:1-3
Matthew, 1:1-16 and 1:18-25
Luke, 1:26-35
Acts, 2:36
Luke, 2:11
John, 13:13
Ephesians, 1:20-22
John, 6:38
John, 8:58
Philippians, 2:5-11
Colossians, 1:15-16
Hebrews, 1:1-3

Session four

John, 3:17
Luke, 9:31
Matthew, 26:39 and 26:42
Romans, 5:6
Galatians, 1:4
John, 1:29
Romans, 5:10
Romans, 6:3-11
1 Corinthians, 15:3
Isaiah, 52:13 to 53:12
Ephesians, 1:7
Colossians, 1:22

Hebrews, 1:14
1 Peter, 1:18-19
1 Peter, 2:24
1 John, 1:7
1 John, 2:2
Revelation, 1:5
Romans, 5:9
Romans, 5:1
John, 3:18
Romans, 8:1
Colossians, 2:14
Romans, 6:1-23
John, 1:12-13
2 Corinthians, 5:17
Ephesians, 2:1-10
Colossians, 3:1
Hebrews, 2:11-18
1 John, 1:8 to 2:2.

Session five

Mark, 1:15
Acts, 17:30
Acts, 3:19
Acts, 26:20
Matthew, 18:3
Matthew, 28:19
Acts, 2:38 and 41
Acts, 8:12 and 36
Acts, 9:18
Acts, 10:47-48
Acts, 16:15 and 33
Acts, 19:5
Ezekiel, 36:25
John, 3:5
1 Peter, 3:20-21

Colossians, 2:12 and 20
Colossians, 3:1
Romans, 10:9-10
Acts, 16:30-31
John, 1:12
John, 3:16-18 and 3:36
John, 5:24
John, 6:35-40
2 Corinthians, 5:17
Colossians, 1:13-14
Revelation, 3:20
Acts, 2:38-39
Luke, 11:9-13
Acts, 10:44-48
Acts, 8:14-17
Acts, 19:5-6
Romans, 5:5
I John, 3:24
Romans, 8:14-17
Galatians, 4:6
Ephesians, 1:13-14
2 Corinthians, 1:22
2,Corinthians, 5:5
Acts, 1:8
Romans, 8:24
John, 14:16 and 14:26
John, 15:26
John, 16:7
Ephesians, 1:17-19.

Session six

John, 6:38-59
Matthew, 28:9
Luke, 23:55 - 24:3
Luke, 24:30-31 and 24:36-43

John, 20:14-30
1 Corinthians, 15:1-20 and 15:38-58
Philippians, 3:21
Hebrews, 1:12
2 Peter, 3:10-15
Revelation, 21:1-8
Acts, 1:10-11
Matthew, 24:3, 24:36, 24:42 and 24:44
Mark, 13:35-36
1 Thessalonians, 5:2-3
Revelation, 1:7
Mark, 13:24-26
Matthew, 24:27
1 Thessalonians, 4:13-18
1 Corinthians, 15:51-52
Matthew, 24:31
Matthew, 25:31-46
2 Thessalonians, 1:6-10
Matthew, 13:40-43 and 13:49-50
Revelation, 20:11-15
John, 5:28-29
John, 6:39, 6:40 and 6:54.

Session seven

John, 15:5
Romans, 12:4-10
1 Corinthians, 12:12-30
Ephesians, 1:23
Ephesians, 4:4 and 4:16
Ephesians, 5:23, 5:29-30
Hebrews, 10:25
Hebrews, 3:13
Acts, 2:42-47
Matthew, 18:20.

Session eight

1 Corinthians, 11:23-26
Matthew, 26:26-29
Mark, 14:22-25
Luke, 22:14-19
Acts, 2:14-19
John, 6:35-59
1 Corinthians, 10:16-17
1 Corinthians, 11:27-32
Matthew, 5:21-24.

Session ten

1 Thessalonians, 5:23
Hebrews, 4:12
John, 3
Ephesians, 2:1-10
1 John, 5:12
Matthew, 4:4
1 Corinthians, 12
Ephesians, 4:11-14
1 Corinthians, 14:3
Genesis, 1:3, 1:6, 1:9, and 1:14
Isaiah, 55:11
1 Peter, 1:23
2 Peter, 3:5-7
Galatians, 4:6
Psalm 139

APPENDIX 2

If, after reading this book you would like to invite Jesus to be the Lord of your life, to be your Saviour and your best friend, here's a suggested prayer.

"Dear Lord Jesus, thank You that You died for my sins. I know that I have sinned. I am truly sorry. Please forgive me. I repent from my sinful ways. Come into my life by Your Spirit. Guide me and help me to be the person You always intended me to be. Amen."

Don't stop with a prayer. Tell a Christian friend that you are now a Christian. Ask them to pray for you. Don't try to be a lone Christian. Join a church. Ask Jesus to show you which church is the right one for you. He will. Remember, nothing is impossible for Him!